Airlift and Airborne Operations in World War II

Roger E. Bilstein

Enhanced with Text Analytics by PageKicker Robot "Fast Hans"

Copyright 2013 Nimble Books LLC

Printed in the United States of America

ISBN-13: 978-1608880416

∞ The paper used in print versions of this publication meets the minimum requirements of the American National Standard for Information Sciences—Permanence of Paper for Printed Library Materials, ANSI Z39.48-1992. The paper is acid-free and lignin-free.

Readability Report

Flesh-Kincaid Grade Level: 12.37

Flesh Reading Ease Score: 41.24

Sentences: 903

Words: 17,663

Average Syllables per Word: 1.72

Average Words per Sentence: 19.56

Dramatis Personae:

Lt. Col. James M. Gavin
General Arnold
Gen. Anthony C. McAuliffe
Capt. Ira Eaker

Gazetteer:

United States
United Air
Europe
Germany
China
France
North Atlantic
Mediterranean
Burma
Himalayas
Sicily
India
Philippines
China-Burma-India
South Atlantic
America

Miscellany:

World War II
U.S. Army Air Forces
Air Transport Command
Air Service
assault
bombers
World War
Northwest Airlines
General Headquarters Air Force
ATC
CBI
Military Airlift Command
U.S. Army
Air Force
AAF
President
Great Britain
Boeing
Airborne Operations
Air Corps
Assault
Air Corps Tactical School
Air Transport
Eighth Air Force
Airborne Division
82d Airborne Division
principal

Airborne
War Department
TWA

Summary

- In the wake of rapid German military successes that began with the invasion of Poland in the autumn of 1939 and culminated with the fall of France in the spring of 1940, a flood of aircraft orders from Britain inundated suppliers in the United States.
- As the survey observed, "the terrain of Burma and China and the absence of land lines of communication forced all agencies in the theater to turn to the airplane—initially as an afterthought and an emergency last-chance measure." The flexibility of air transportation offered planners a unique tool "to meet the exigencies of the various situations." Summing up, the survey declared that "air transport operations expanded beyond the wildest predictions of 1942—expanded because it was the one agency which could succeed." Regarding the CBI theater, the military situation in 1942 appeared to be highly unfavorable.
- The Army Air Forces in World War II.

These are the most statistically representative sentences over 30 characters in length extracted by PageKicker's Text Analysis Tools.

Dramatis Personae:

Lt. Col. James M. Gavin
General Arnold
Gen. Anthony C. McAuliffe
Capt. Ira Eaker

Gazetteer:

United States
United Air
Europe
Germany
China
France
North Atlantic
Mediterranean
Burma
Himalayas
Sicily
India
Philippines
China-Burma-India
South Atlantic
America

Miscellany:

World War II
U.S. Army Air Forces
Air Transport Command
Air Service
assault
bombers
World War
Northwest Airlines
General Headquarters Air Force
ATC
CBI
Military Airlift Command
U.S. Army
Air Force
AAF
President
Great Britain
Boeing
Airborne Operations
Air Corps
Assault
Air Corps Tactical School
Air Transport
Eighth Air Force
Airborne Division
82d Airborne Division
principal

The U.S. Army Air Forces in World War II

Airlift and Airborne Operations in World War II

Roger E. Bilstein

AIR FORCE HISTORY AND MUSEUMS PROGRAM
1998

Airlift and Airborne Operations in World War II

As World War II unfolded in Europe during the late 1930s and early 1940s, U.S. military planners realized the nation's airlift and airborne combat capability was underdeveloped and out of date. The U.S. Army Air Forces relied largely on civil airline equipment and personnel to launch the Air Transport Command's intercontinental routes to overseas combat zones. A separate Troop Carrier Command and newly formed airborne divisions hammered out doctrinal concepts and tactical requirements for paratroop engagements. Despite operational shortcomings, subsequent airborne assaults in North Africa and Italy generated a base of knowledge from which to plan such massive aerial formations and paratroop drops as those for the Normandy invasion and Operation MARKET-GARDEN, and strategic efforts in the China-Burma-India theater. Airlift routes over the Himalayas demonstrated one of the war's most effective uses of air transport. The Air Transport Command emerged as a remarkably successful organization with thousands of aircraft and a global network of communications centers, weather forecasting offices, airfields, and maintenance depots, and air-age realities influenced a postwar generation of dedicated military air transports operating around the world.

Contents

Introduction 1

Early Airlift and Airborne Units 7

Pilots and Airplanes 13

      DC–3/C–47 15

      C–46 17

      C–87 19

      C–54 and C–69 20

      Helicopters 23

      Gliders 24

Airborne Operations in the Mediterranean 27

Special Missions 30

      FRANTIC 30

      CARPETBAGGER and the Balkans 31

The Assault on Europe 31

      OVERLORD 31

      MARKET-GARDEN 33

      Bastogne and VARSITY 36

Flying the Hump 38

Other Far East Missions 43

Legacies 45

Suggested Reading 50

INTRODUCTION

Following the entry of the United States into World War I in the spring of 1917, the aviation units in the Signal Corps explored the possibilities of employing aircraft for military transport. Although the 1916 Pershing Expedition into Mexico occasionally had used airplanes for reconnaissance and to carry mail and dispatches, the equipment available during that operation proved unreliable. In 1918, the Signal Corps supplied airplanes and pilots to inaugurate the first U.S. airmail service, an operation expected to help train pilots and boost airplane production. This experiment did little for either goal, and the Post Office Department soon took complete control. Overseas, aircraft based in France sometimes carried a single officer or courier, or perhaps priority military dispatches, but the available single-engine, two-place airplanes permitted little else.

An effort to assist a force of 500 U.S. soldiers surrounded by the Germans during the Argonne Forest campaign in October 1918 achieved very little. Remembered as the "Lost Battalion," the American unit recovered almost none of the supplies that U.S. airplanes dropped near its position. However, the beleaguered troops surmised the need to mark their location for better identification from the air, and the panels they laid out provided needed information to pinpoint their position and allow relief forces to fight through to them. The object lesson of aerial marking became standard procedure.

Before the end of the war, Brig. Gen. William Mitchell had begun plans for a massive aerial offensive against Germany that would rely on Allied use of extensive bombing as well as tactical air strikes. Mitchell's planned aerial assault, moreover, included dramatic use of airborne forces. He proposed an airdrop of an entire U.S. infantry division behind the German lines, using Handley-Page bombers from the British Royal Air Force (RAF), followed by subsequent air cargo missions by the bombers to support these airborne units with ammunition and other supplies. The U.S. high command had this remarkable gambit under serious consideration when World War I ended abruptly in November 1918. Mitchell's concept clearly anticipated tactics used some twenty-two years later in the Second World War.

Hampered by parsimonious budgets and deteriorating equipment in the postwar era, planners had little opportunity to implement comprehensive plans like Mitchell's. There were some bright spots, such as the Model Airways system, which operated from 1922 to 1926. Sponsored by several forward-thinking officers in the new Air Service, the Model Airways linked Bolling Field in Washington, D.C., with a number of military airfields scattered across several midwestern states, down to Kelly and Brooks Fields in Texas. During the few years of its existence, the Air Service evolved a regularly scheduled mail and cargo service, as well as ad hoc operations. Equipment varied: available airplanes designated as cargo

An air route map for the Model Airway System.

On the schedule board in this Model Airway System's operations room, one flight is shown delayed for seven days because of weather. The system linked several U.S. military airfields from 1922 to 1926.

types were used and an occasional bomber was pressed into service. During its four-year history, the Model Airways completed several hundred flights and moved over sixty thousand pounds of cargo and more than 650 passengers. Federal legislation for commercial airmail service in 1925, coupled with specific restrictions on competing services under the Air Corps Act of 1926, put an end to the Model Airways. Its legacy of operational and logistical planning experience, however, proved to be a useful one.

Miscellaneous air cargo activities took place during the 1920s and 1930s and the U.S. Army conducted limited exercises using parachutists, but doctrinal emphasis on bombardment and on aerial combat meant that comparatively less attention was expended on airlift concepts. Nonetheless, maneuvers during the late 1920s and early 1930s kept the idea alive and under discussion at the Air Corps Tactical School. The drawbacks of this limited approach became all too clear when the U.S. Army attempted to provide the nation's airmail service during the late winter of 1934.

Domestic commercial air service, meanwhile, had made impressive progress by the mid-1930s. Private companies became skilled at developing airmail routes supported by requisite scheduling and logistical support. Passenger flying evolved during the early 1930s, along with improved aircraft and navigational equipment. Although not able to fly in every kind of weather or night conditions, the commercial airlines offered

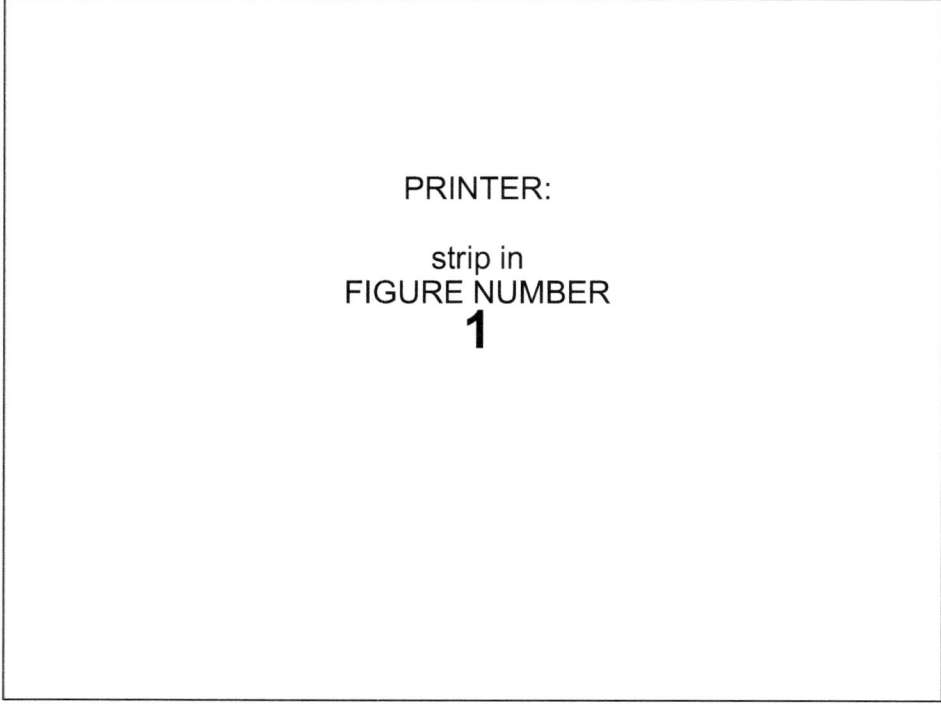

In May 1918, the first U.S. airmail service included a letter from President Woodrow Wilson to the governor of New York.

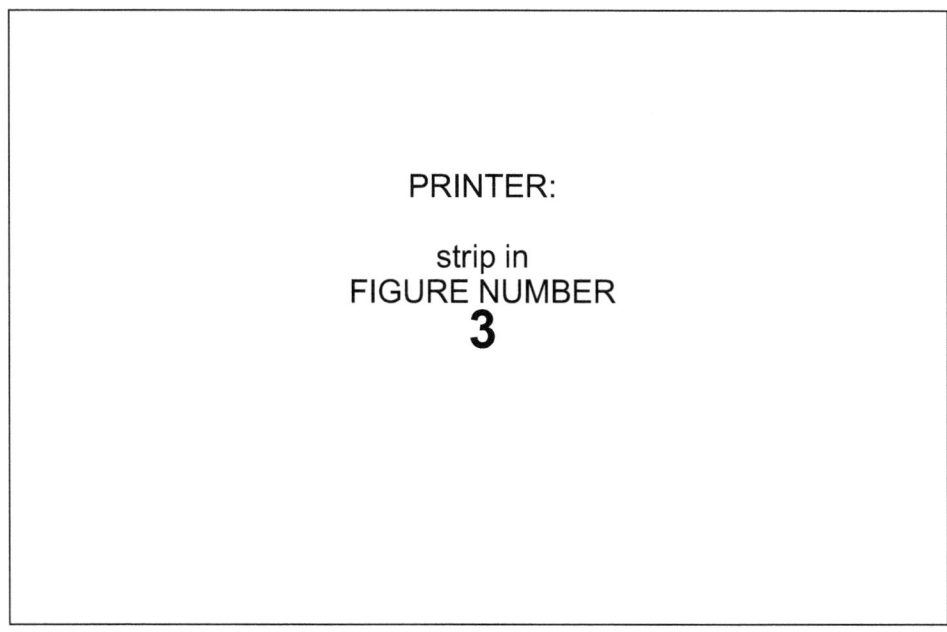

Gen. Oscar Westover (left) and Col. James E. Chaney stand before a map of airmail service routes.

a valuable transportation service for that era. Early in 1934, questions about the legality of certain airmail contracts prompted federal action to cancel all of the current contracts and to rely on the Air Corps to fly the mail. The Air Corps confidently responded, on the basis of its earlier experience with cargo, maneuvers, and long-range navigation exercises for its bomber squadron—all of which, however, had taken place in favorable weather. Flying conditions during the early months of 1934 were actually abominable; a flurry of sixty-six crashes killed twelve Air Corps pilots trying to fly the mail. In the aftermath, improved training, weather forecasting, and navigational technology for transport duties were developed.

Despite the embarrassing airmail venture, officers interested in aviation remembered earlier events that argued for a modern airlift capability. Among them was an emergency airlift mounted in 1916 to support a British garrison under siege by Turkish troops in Mesopotamia. A handful of single-engine RAF biplanes managed to drop several thousand pounds of supplies over a period of two weeks before Turkish forces defeated a relief column and the British surrendered. The RAF mounted a somewhat different sort of airlift during late 1928 and early 1929, when biplane transports successfully evacuated nearly six hundred people and twenty-four thousand pounds of belongings from Kabul, Afghanistan, during a period of tribal unrest. These operations dramatically illustrated airlift's capabilities to transfer large numbers of personnel and cargo. Closer to home, from 1927 to 1929, U.S. Marines operating in Nicaragua used trimotor Fokker and Ford transports to carry troops, equipment, and dispatches. The Marines also used these aircraft for medical evacuation and to air-drop supplies to armed patrols deep in the Central American jungles. With this background and an awareness of airlift sharpened by the recent airmail experience, essential changes began to occur.

A reorganization of the Army Air Corps gave more authority to transport functions, including authorization for modern, twin-engine transport airplanes. In 1936, the Air Corps bought twenty new Douglas DC–2 trans-

Airmail pilots Maj. Reuben H. Fleet and Lt. George L. Boyle review aerial routes for the Washington-to-New York trip.

An early ground crew helps Lt. George L. Boyle take off from Washington, D.C., on the return leg of the first airmail flight.

Capt. Ira Eaker survived a crash in his Boeing Hornet Shuttle. The Model 95 mail plane, modified to a two-seat configuration that could be refueled in midair, made several nonstop transcontinental flights in the 1920s.

ports, designating them C–33s and C–34s. The following year, the 10th Transport Group emerged as the first permanent logistics unit, replacing several provisional units that had come and gone over previous years. Additionally, General Headquarters Air Force (GHQ Air Force) built up its own tactical support. This sort of split in resources persisted as a source of contention for nearly a decade as various commands competed for air transport assets, especially in World War II. In any case, the total number of dedicated transport airplanes of useful capacity remained inadequate. Against proposals for about 150 airplanes in the late 1930s, only 30 additional DC–2 types entered service through 1939.

Moreover, the Air Corps had no large, four-engine transports for transoceanic missions. Compared with the record of commercial airlines, the inability of the U.S. military services to deploy intercontinental airlift was embarrassing. Following the first transatlantic flights of 1919, the development of commercial services required nearly two decades. Nonetheless, by the late 1930s, European countries like Britain, Holland, and France had pioneered impressive route systems throughout the continent, over the Mediterranean, and across the Middle East to various colonies in the Pacific region. The French and Germans operated airmail services across the South Atlantic between Africa and Brazil, on the South American coast. In the United States, federal support for Pan American Airways helped transform it into an intercontinental aerial system. By the late 1930s, Pan Am not only delivered mail and passengers throughout Latin America but also had inaugurated similar operations across the Pacific and Atlantic Oceans.

Still, the majority of these efforts operated on a seasonal basis, required several days at a time, kept to a limited schedule of only one or two flights a week, and were beyond the means of all but the wealthiest travelers. Pan Am's longest routes relied on big, four-engine flying boats built by Martin and Boeing. Another U.S. airline, Transcontinental and Western Air—later Trans World Airlines—(TWA), had introduced four-engine Boeing Stratoliner passenger transports on important domestic routes. Pressurized for high-altitude flights, they were in the forefront of modern airliner design.

Building on this legacy of U.S. airline experience and using commercial aircraft, the Army's early, long-range airlift gained an invaluable advantage. During the course of World War II, having built numerous weather stations and hundreds of airfields around the world in only a few years, the Army Air Forces commanded a large fleet of long-range transports that flew intercontinental schedules as a matter of course. That effort would provoke a postwar revolution in air transportation.

EARLY AIRLIFT AND AIRBORNE UNITS

The meteoric growth of airlift capability during the Second World War had its origins in requirements for delivering aircraft to France and Great Britain on the eve of hostilities, as well as in the need to establish rapid, secure lines of transportation to friendly nations under enemy threat in distant areas of the world. The Air Corps Ferrying Command (ACFC) and the Air Transport Command (ATC) emerged in this first wave of development. The rush of events included changes in nomenclature when the War Department established the U.S. Army Air Forces (AAF) on June 20, 1941, to control both the Army Air Corps and the Air Force Combat Command.

In the wake of rapid German military successes that began with the invasion of Poland in the autumn of 1939 and culminated with the fall of France in the spring of 1940, a flood of aircraft orders from Britain inundated suppliers in the United States. British and French aircraft orders had already sparked significant production increases dating from 1938. Amendments to the American neutrality legislation of the 1930s made it possible for Great Britain to obtain critical war matériel on a cash-and-carry basis, but the British government began to run short of money by the end of 1940. Searching for a means to contain the spread of Axis influence, support Britain in this cause, and respond to the erosion of Britain's treasury, the Roosevelt administration hit upon the idea of Lend-Lease. The Lend-Lease Act, passed by Congress in March 1941, authorized production of combat equipment for loan to Britain, with the equipment to be returned when the military emergency ended. Although naval convoys could probably get much equipment past attacks by German U-boats in the Atlantic, the difficulties of transporting large numbers of aircraft by sea presented a special problem. For a time, civilian pilots flew airplanes purchased by Great Britain across the U.S. border into Canada, where other civilians, under British contracts, piloted them across the North Atlantic to airfields in Scotland. As the air war intensified over the United Kingdom, many civilian pilots became reluctant to fly into the war zone, and others were drafted into the RAF, creating serious bottlenecks in the flow of aircraft. General Henry H. "Hap" Arnold, chief of the U.S. Army Air Corps, argued that U.S. military pilots could do the job while acquiring valuable flying experience and easing pressure on the British. This bold step also placed U.S. fliers in an increasingly active war zone.

The Air Corps Ferrying Command, created on May 29, 1941, immediately began flying airplanes to Newfoundland. The new organization expanded operations during July, delivering 1,350 aircraft to Great Britain by December 7, 1941. In addition, the ACFC inaugurated an emergency, transatlantic transportation service for key personnel, high-priority cargo, and diplomatic correspondence. The first operations began on July 1, 1941, when a four-engine B–24 bomber flew a Washington-Montreal-Newfoundland-Scotland mission. Within a few weeks, the "Arnold Line," as military personnel called it, scheduled at least six round-trips each month, a frequency that persisted until interrupted by hazardous winter weather over the Atlantic. By the end of 1941, authorization from the White House officially allowed the ACFC to operate far-flung routes on a global basis, a process that had already begun to evolve in response to other requirements related to Lend-Lease agreements.

When Germany invaded the Soviet Union on June 22, 1941, the United States extended Lend-Lease to that nation as well. To assist the Soviets, one aerial route ran north across Canada and through Alaska to Siberia. Deliveries to Britain continued to move across the North Atlantic. Another important new aerial route assisted Britain in North Africa, and extended across the Near East to reach southwestern points of the Soviet Union. Planes on such flights moved southward to Brazil, then eastward across the South Atlantic into Africa. A diverging route on this southern airway also supported Allied efforts in India and Australia, where Japanese pressures increased. Because many northern and central ocean passages in the Pacific were under threat from Japan, the South Atlantic operations became a crucial supply line for aircraft and supplies to the China-Burma-India (CBI) theater. At the same time, a tenuous air-route system reached from the U.S. west coast into the South Pacific to Australia, making the Army Air Forces a presence on every continent.

The ACFC solidified these routes, building on the pioneer flights accomplished by commercial operations of the 1930s. The command installed vital meteorological equipment and weather stations and began to erect and furnish maintenance facilities, provide housing for itinerant crews and personnel, and organize the far-flung infrastructure needed to support hundreds of aircraft moving along thousands of miles of airways each day. In all of this, the command relied on the resources of airplanes and personnel in established U.S. airlines.

With so much activity along the segments of the South Atlantic route, the route became one of the first candidates for civil contract work. Beginning in the spring of 1941, Pan American Airways began to handle this task, moving airplanes across the Caribbean and down the eastern coast of South America to Natal, Brazil. From there, three principal airways went to Africa's western coast. Most of that air traffic then winged across central Africa to the Sudan, from which point other routes spread through the Middle East and across India. Pan Am's experience in the Caribbean and South America ensured recognition of local customs and supported the need to obtain supplies from local sources. By the end of 1942, Pan Am had delivered about 460 airplanes over this southern air transport system.

During 1942, many other airlines became contractors for ferrying aircraft around the world. Northeast, along with TWA, flew missions over North Atlantic routes. New schedules from the United States to Alaska were flown by Northwest Airlines, Western Air Lines, and United Air Lines. Additional U.S. carriers signed on during the war, implementing services through Central and South America as well as within the continental United States. During 1942, the airlines and their crews performed nearly 88 percent of the military's ferrying and airlift activities. By the end of the war, military transports and personnel predominated, although contractors still did as much as 19 percent of the work.

At the same time that worldwide air routes were being hammered out, military leaders overhauled the Army's organizational structure. During the spring of 1941, the General Staff thoroughly revamped the air services, creating the U.S. Army Air Forces in June 1941. General Arnold became chief of the new AAF, guiding it through succeeding organizational changes. After the Japanese attacked Pearl Harbor on December 7, 1941, change became the order of the day. Germany declared war against the United States a few days later and, among many challenges, the AAF forged its aerial support network into military air routes around the world.

Early in 1942, Arnold authorized an Air Service Command to handle all aerial transport among U.S. bases within the Western Hemisphere. This command also received responsibility for providing airlift for infantry, gliders, and paratroop units. The Ferrying Command was charged with delivering aircraft and providing air transport services outside the Western Hemisphere. As a history of the Military Airlift Command noted later, the separation of troop carrier operations from long-range air logistics marked "a watershed in a doctrinal issue" (p. 18). The Ferrying Command was a single command with global responsibilities, and its mission, and that of its successors, "represented the logical development of these doctrinal ideals."

When U.S. military forces transferred overseas in the course of wartime deployments, an issue of theater precedence created awkward confrontations. Traditionally, theater commanders could claim all the military resources within their areas. Consequently, when a Ferrying Command flight en route to some further destination landed in an overseas combat zone, theater commanders desperate for equipment often tried to commandeer such aircraft for their own purposes. These confrontations continued to occur for the duration of the war despite efforts of the General Staff to rein in their theater officers and despite further refinements in nomenclature, roles, and missions.

Another issue evolved from the role of the Naval Air Transport System, which was hastily organized after Pearl Harbor to offer rapid transportation of dispatches and personnel to remote naval installations around the world and to supply rapid logistical support for critical, lightweight items required by far-flung units of the fleet. For these tasks, the Navy collected an assortment of land and sea airplanes, after pressing into service long-range flying boats originally intended for patrol and rescue duties. High-level planners in Washington—civilian as well as military—began to lobby for a unified military air service operation to achieve maximum use of available aircraft. When the United States became an official combatant on December 7, 1941, having military personnel in charge of aircraft whose operations took them into active combat zones became imperative.

On June 20, 1942, Arnold issued AAF General Orders that responded to these issues and set the pattern for most of the war's duration. This included creation of the Air Transport Command, which was responsible for all ferrying requirements within the United States and overseas. Additionally, the ATC was authorized to transport all personnel, mail, and matériel for the War Department, with the exception of specific combat commands who had their own aircraft. The ATC also assumed the task of running all overseas airways, including facilities, communication, support, and related requirements. The Air Service Command retained only its continental flying tasks. The new Troop Carrier Command became the focus of airborne combat operations and ad hoc air transport within operational theaters. Although the Navy continued to operate its own Naval Air Transport Service, a committee within the Joint Chiefs of Staff exercised more unified control toward the end of the war. This bureaucratic element (the Joint Army-Navy Air Transport Committee) helped focus plans to create a single airlift command after World War II.

Meanwhile, the Japanese attack on Pearl Harbor had triggered an immediate need for many more airplanes and pilots. Early in 1942, the Army's air transport resources included only eleven four-engine airplanes, converted B–24 Liberator bombers. In addition, there arose a severe shortage of modern transports like the DC–2 conversions. Fortunately, the means to fill this gap already existed, owing to the foresight of Edgar Gorrell, president of the Air Transport Association (ATA), the trade organization for major airlines in the United States.

With military approval, the civil airline fleet of the United States already had an operational blueprint in case of a national emergency like war. Gorrell, a veteran of the U.S. Air Service in World War I, recognized the potential military value of the growing airline fleet of cargo airplanes, and had begun planning for an aerial mobilization as early as 1936 with the cooperation of the "Big Four" of the airline industry (American, Eastern, TWA, and United). Assisted by Air Corps officers, he had updated the plans over the years and included options for effective disposition of airplanes, flight crews, and ground personnel on twenty-four hours' notice. When Pearl Harbor was bombed, Gorrell had a program ready for implementation. The Gorrell blueprint was enthusiastically embraced by C.R. Smith of American Airlines and by General Arnold, and helped to form the nucleus of the ATC.

As the Ferrying Command became the basis for a worldwide air transport system, Arnold and other AAF leaders prudently decided to bring in someone with prior experience in managing the large flotilla of aircraft, complex scheduling, and thousands of personnel bound to grow to even larger proportions. A veteran of civil operations could also do a better job of molding these Air Transport Association assets. In 1942, C. R. Smith became a colonel in the ATC as deputy commander to the ATC chief, Brig. Gen. Harold Lee George. All of the ATA carriers in the United States had to make the best of stripped-down fleets and reduced schedules. American's own Flagship Fleet dropped from 79 to 41 airplanes; overall, the total number of ATA civil airliners in the United States dropped to 176 from a total of 359. The airline industry did its best to meet civilian demands during the war by squeezing more air time out of each remaining airplane. In the case of American Airlines, Smith's residual management team elicited 30 percent more flying hours each year, compared with a typical prewar year.

In the meantime, Smith settled into his job as the operations chief for the ATC. At the beginning of the war, the preferred route to the European theater still ran across the South Atlantic, from Natal, Brazil, to Dakar, Senegal. Smith listened carefully to those who argued for a regularized North Atlantic crossing, flying the Great Circle route from Newfoundland via Greenland and Iceland, to Great Britain. He authorized a technical staff and a survey flight in a former American DC–3 using American personnel. Having proved the feasibility of North Atlantic service on a regular basis, the ATC soon launched dozens of similar ferry and cargo flights.

While General George and C. R. Smith at ATC contended with cargo flights and ferrying duties, the Troop Carrier Command (TCC) began to evolve. As the first U.S. effort at airborne combat operations for paratroops and glider troops, its creation resulted directly from events in wartime Europe.

During the spring of 1940, German forces invaded Denmark and Norway, using aerial assault units in a series of successful parachute and cargo-airplane operations to seize key positions and then relying on aerial resupply until more substantial forces joined up. U.S. strategists took notice. German aerial units also attacked advanced strong points in the German sweep through the low countries and into France. These actions involved parachutists as well as glider troops. U.S. observers followed these operations even more keenly because the battles in Europe made it clear that airborne operations had become an integral factor of modern warfare. Then, in the spring of 1941, Germany's aerial assault on the British island of Crete in the Mediterranean combined paratroops, gliders, and the use of air transports to carry the offensive completely. The U.S. military appeared to lag seriously in this new art of warfare.

During the summer of 1940, the U.S. Army had taken its first steps toward developing paratroop forces and planning for airborne assaults. Germany's aerial invasion of Crete accelerated preparations for field exercises, which included airborne units scheduled for long-overdue, full-scale maneuvers. Conducted in Louisiana, these exercises revealed that the U.S. armed forces were unprepared for modern war. Troop formations included soldiers equipped with broom handles to represent machine guns and automobiles fitted with stove pipes wheeled around to portray tank units. The recently formed 50th Transport Wing scraped together a polyglot force of thirty-nine airplanes for the occasion and managed to stage the U.S. Army's first airdrop with more than one company of paratroopers in a single operation. Much more needed to be accomplished, and the time to do it was short.

Working rapidly in the aftermath of Pearl Harbor, the Army created a new Airborne Command with two components, the 82d and the 101st Airborne Divisions. The chief architect for subsequent airborne missions was Lt. Col. James M. Gavin, a commander from the 82d Airborne Division. Gavin, a student of the recent European experiences in airborne attack, was also informed by the difficulties experienced during the Louisiana maneuvers. Basically he focused on the need to drop paratroops as a cohesive, concentrated force. With enough airplanes, Gavin argued, a major airborne assault could achieve substantial victories and pave the way for the rapid advance of conventional ground troops. In the process of additional training and maneuvers, the 82d Airborne established a standard jump altitude of six hundred feet—high enough to reduce injuries and low enough to concentrate the jumpers in a compact area as a cohesive fighting force. Using formations of thirty-six to forty-five transports like the C–47 (the military version of the DC–3), it was possible to insert a battalion in two minutes and drop a regiment in ten minutes. Typically, mission planners picked a jump zone within a few miles of enemy positions where paratroops could seize a key area behind the lines and hold it until Allied forces broke through to meet them. These principles formed the basis for fourteen major airborne assaults by U.S. forces during the Second World War. In addition, numerous smaller actions and reinforcement missions took place in every theater of the war.

PILOTS AND AIRPLANES

The search for qualified pilots intensified in 1942. Early on, the Ferrying Command scoured the country for all available civilian fliers; bush pilots, test pilots, crop dusters, stunt pilots, barnstormers, and pilots who flew on personal business or for fun all became candidates. These draftees were expected to have five hundred hours of flying experience, a requirement that soon dropped to two hundred to three hundred hours, depending on the military's need. If they could pass a ninety-day probation period, they became commissioned officers. By the end of 1942, a total of 1,372 pilots had been commissioned, but the AAF's own flight-training programs began to replace these conscripts after that date.

Several hundred women also served, largely as the result of urgent needs by the ATC and the philosophy that women could take over ferrying operations to release more men for active combat assignments. Special recruitment and training procedures eventually evolved into an organization called the Women's Airforce Service Pilots (WASPs), until it was inactivated at the end of 1944. Even though not eligible for commissions, and frequently hampered by bureaucratic shortsightedness, the WASPs performed with great professionalism. A total of 303 served as ferry pilots within the continental United States, and their twenty-seven months of active duty involved delivery or movement of 12,650 aircraft, from bombers and fighters to two-place trainers.

Just as civil personnel formed the nucleus of ATC's pilot ranks, civil aircraft performed its missions. These civil airplanes included the nation's most advanced transports—all of them, in fact. In mid-December 1941, when the War Department desperately sought to expand its force of four-engine transport aircraft, the only such airplanes in military service included the eleven B–24s used by the Ferrying Command, plus one Boeing 314 Clipper flying boat purchased from Pan Am in August. The only other large, four-engine transports available numbered fifteen, all in civil airline service, including Pan Am's eight additional Clippers and two Martin M–130 flying boats. TWA had five land-based Boeing 307 Stratoliners, a land-based transport equipped with a pressurized cabin, making it one of the most advanced transports of the era. The government bought them all under a national emergency decree, and parceled them out to the services. The two Martin flying boats and five Clippers went to the Navy; the Army received the three remaining Clippers, along with TWA's five Stratoliners. That gave the AAF a total of twenty four-engine aircraft—hardly enough

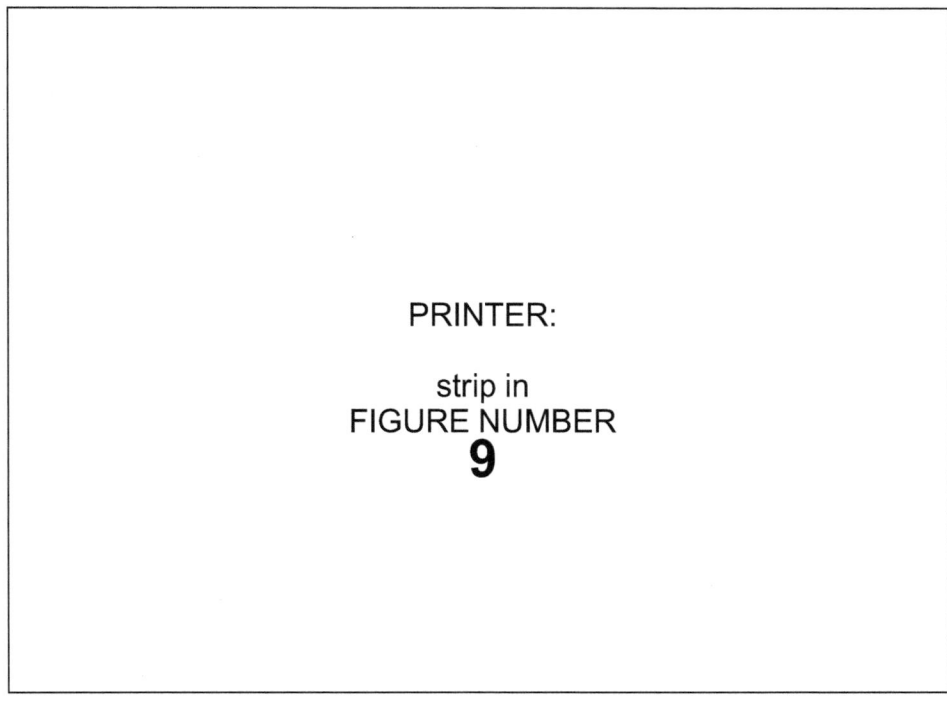

Three of the 303 ferry pilots in the Women's Airforce Service Pilots (WASPs), an organization that delivered more than twelve thousand aircraft.

with which to fight a war. The AAF scrambled to fill the gap with many more types adapted from civilian designs.

During the 1920s and 1930s, the Army's air transport organization had acquired only a few dozen airplanes under the cargo designation. In the mid-1920s, the service purchased eleven Fokker trimotor transports, designated C–2, along with thirteen Ford trimotors, designated C–3, C–4, and C–9. The service also operated about two dozen Douglas Dolphin twin-engine amphibians, useful in miscellaneous duties in the Philippines and the Panama Canal Zone and for occasional coastal patrols. But for two decades after World War I, little progress occurred with respect to later AAF equipment, operational experience, or coherent doctrine for large-scale airlift actions.

During 1941, as U.S. planners began to think seriously about the role of air transport in time of national emergency, no one completely grasped the potential role of airlift as a major means of supplying military forces. Eventually, by the late summer of 1942, the backlog of cargoes awaiting shipment overseas brought home the importance of intercontinental air transport. The backlog not only made it clear that many more airplanes were needed immediately, but also underscored their potential for future use. At that point, according to the official history of the United States Air

Force in World War II, "the idea of air transport as a major instrument of logistics [began] to take shape."

When the United States became fully involved in World War II, aircraft of all types were drafted into military service and given new designations. They ranged from personal airplanes like the Fairchild F–24 (redesignated C–61) to twin-engine Lockheed Lodestar airline transports (C–60 designation, plus others). The AAF also pressed into service the sole examples of experimental long-range bombers such as the Boeing XB–17, which made several cargo flights as the XC–105, and the larger Douglas XB–19, which was modified to carry 123 troops or fifty-six thousand pounds of freight but received no formal cargo designation. These and other airplanes played useful roles, although the lion's share of wartime military transport duties was conducted by four types of aircraft: the Douglas C–47 and C–54; the Curtiss C–46; and the Consolidated C–87, a converted B–24 bomber.

DC–3/C–47

The renowned Douglas DC–3 served in larger numbers than any other wartime transport. Its precursor, the DC–1, originated in 1931 in response to a request from TWA, which wanted to replace trimotored airliners in service at the time. The principal impetus came after a Fokker trimotor went down in a Kansas wheat field killing, among others, Knute Rockne, the famous football coach at Notre Dame University. Public antipathy toward trimotors, including conventional wood-and-fabric construction, spurred the young Douglas company to design a new kind of all-metal twin-engine transport. The airplane's designers also took advantage of advanced aeronautical engineering techniques of the era, including wing flaps, retractable gear, deicing equipment, NACA (National Advisory Committee for Aeronautics) cowling, flush riveting, stressed-skin construction, variable-pitch propellers, and state-of-the-art engines with greater reliability and time before overhaul. The melding of all these and other features resulted in an aircraft that soon played a key role in commercial air transportation. By 1938, it was estimated that 80 percent of all U.S. passengers traveled in DC–3s. Designed and built for commercial airline service but adaptable for other purposes, the DC–3 and other airliners of the same era resulted in a fleet of military transports that compiled a heroic record of wartime service.

The AAF's initial deployment of the DC–3 type actually began with its immediate predecessor, the DC–2, which was the production version of the DC–1. Three variants were eventually purchased and were designated C–32, C–33, and C–39. By 1942, nearly eighty airplanes of all three types had entered service and were capable of carrying fourteen to sixteen passengers. The C–39s, in particular, proved their value early in the war, evacuating large numbers of personnel from the Philippines to Australia

The C–47 Skytrain, affectionately called the Gooney Bird.

and helping to establish an aerial shuttle service from New England to Labrador, thus supporting the demanding routes that continued across the North Atlantic.

In the meantime, Douglas had developed the DC–3 version of its new airliner, equipped with improved engines, aerodynamic refinements, a larger fuselage, and an optional cargo door for handling bulky shipments of air freight. The new DC–3 entered airline service in 1936, beginning a remarkable career. The AAF took first deliveries of this type of aircraft in early 1942, with the designation C–47 Skytrain. The British military service dubbed it the Dakota, and Allied troops around the globe affectionately referred to the airplane as the "Gooney Bird." With Pratt & Whitney engines of 1,200 hp each, the C–47 had a top speed of 220 mph with a maximum range of fifteen hundred miles. Its crew typically consisted of pilot and copilot and usually included a crew chief to oversee cargo handling. The wartime C–47 transports discarded the roomy, twenty-one–seat interiors of the airline version and installed bench seats along the fuselage walls to seat thirty-two passengers or twenty-seven troops in combat gear. Hospital transport conversions carried up to twenty-four stretcher cases, but medical evacuations in wartime carried several dozen wounded in harried evacuation flights. The big cargo door on the port side facilitated handling of military shipments of six thousand pounds in regular operations, although the C–47s lifted thousands more in military emergencies on shorter hops.

A nearly identical DC–3 variant, the C–53 Skytrooper, lacked the cargo door and went into service as a troop carrier equipped to haul forty-two passengers or twenty-six fully equipped paratroopers. The AAF acquired 378 Skytroopers, and about two hundred more DC–3 types taken from the airlines entered service as the C–48 through C–52, as well as others. All of these shared the basic airframe of the C–47, differing only in seating arrangements, engines, and other details. At a distance, each

These rows of gasoline tanks were loaded onto C–47s to resupply frontline forces.

appeared so similar that reporters and military personnel tended to lump them all under the generic designation C–47.

The ubiquity of the Skytrain-Dakota-Gooney Bird transport, and its ability to operate from very rough forward airstrips, made it familiar to millions of Allied forces stationed around the world. The C–47 and its relatives not only pioneered in-theater wartime routes but also served as VIP transports, general personnel transports, troop carriers, glider tugs, paratroop assault transports, cargo transports, airborne ambulances, air-sea rescue craft, and special operations aircraft. Supporters of the airplane liked to quote a remark attributed to Gen. Dwight D. Eisenhower: "Four things won the Second World War—the bazooka, the Jeep, the atom bomb, and the C–47 Gooney Bird." By war's end, some thirteen thousand C–47 variants had been delivered, plus two thousand more built under license by foreign manufacturers. The C–47 played a major role in postwar service, remaining in operational units through the 1960s; in the late 1960s, as the AC–47 Gunship, the redoubtable Douglas transports conducted strafing missions during the war in Vietnam.

C–46

The Curtiss C–46 Commando originated in 1940 as a large, thirty-six–passenger airliner, clearly intended to leapfrog the successful Douglas DC–3. As a bigger, potentially more productive twin-engine military

The Curtiss C–46 Commando was a heavily used workhorse in every theater of the Second World War.

transport, the C–46 was quickly taken over by military authorities at the outbreak of World War II. The C–46 eventually served in every theater of the war, although it became most closely associated with operations over the "Hump" in the China-Burma-India theater. Its Pratt & Whitney engines, rated at 2,000 hp each, gave it a top speed of 260 mph. The airplane's range of nearly three thousand miles with a combat load of sixteen thousand pounds made it a heavily used workhorse; it also carried fifty combat troops or thirty-three litter patients for medical evacuation. The airplane's size and cargo load justified a three-man crew, including pilot, copilot, and crew chief, with an occasional cabin assistant or extra cargo loader as needed. The C–46 entered service in 1942, and combat operations quickly resulted in a host of variants to meet rapidly changing combat conditions and specialized loads. Wartime production totaled 3,180 basic models.

Early experience with the C–46 saddled it with a poor reputation. Beset at first by hydraulic failures and related problems, it became known as a "plumber's nightmare." The C–46 was temperamental to fly; its instability at slow speeds made it unsuitable for airdrop missions at low altitudes, and loading the aircraft called for a careful distribution of weights and balance. But despite an initial distaste for the C–46 among ATC aircrews, it soon gained devoted adherents. Aircrews came to appreciate its big cargo doors and roomy fuselage. The C–46 had excellent visibility, comfortable seats that were adjustable, and power-assisted hydraulic controls that eased pilot strain on long missions. Factory design changes and operational experience mitigated a spate of early complaints about engines and pesky maintenance problems as crews integrated the C–46 into their military duties.

C–87

Even before twin-engine military transports demonstrated their indispensability during World War II, the AAF took steps to acquire larger, four-engine aircraft as cargo transports. During 1940–41, responding to overseas tensions and the pressing requirements of Lend-Lease operations, the Army Ferrying Command took shape and decided to operate the modified Consolidated B–24 Liberator bomber. Designated B–24A, the airplane was stripped of bomb-bay gear and assigned to long-distance routes, where its top speed of 300 mph and range of three thousand miles made it a valued asset. With its high, shoulder-mounted wing, boxy fuselage shape, low ground clearance, and extended range, the Liberator seemed a natural design for conversion into a full-time transport.

Production orders for the transport version, the C–87, quickly followed. External changes included the elimination of gun turrets and the bombardier's plexiglass nose position, which was covered over; the addition of seven windows cut into each side of the fuselage and a large cargo door at the rear of the port side; and the elimination of bomb-bay doors. The C–87 carried a five-man crew—pilot, copilot, navigator, radio operator, and crew chief—along with twenty-five passengers or a cargo of twelve thousand pounds in certain conditions. One early variant, the C–87A, came as an executive-style transport equipped with ten berths for oceanic hops and other lengthy missions. There was an armed version, the C–87B, used on flights over the Hump in China where routes brought it close to Japanese fighter bases. The C–109 version also flew over the Hump but was equipped with special containers to carry fuel for B–29 Superfortresses based in China. The production run for the basic C–87 model came to 291 aircraft, although a considerable number of airplanes

The Consolidated C–87, the transport version of the B–24 Liberator bomber, carried a five-man crew and 25 passengers.

underwent conversion to C–87 transport status without carrying the cargo designation. There were also ad hoc uses. In the autumn of 1944, when Gen. George S. Patton's tanks outran fuel supplies in France, the AAF assigned an entire wing of B–24 Liberators from the Eighth Air Force to carry emergency gas to Patton's logistical centers.

C–54 and C–69

The Liberator transport served a useful purpose, but its original design as a bomber did not make it fully compatible with the growing list of wartime personnel transport and cargo needs. In any case, the continuing demand for bombers argued for a different set of production lines to supply a four-engine transport. Fortunately, a new Douglas airliner, the DC–4, seemed to fit the ATC's requirements. Like the B–24, and unlike the "tail draggers" of the day, the DC–4 mounted tricycle landing gear, giving it a horizontal attitude on the flight line. Original specifications for the DC–4 originated with a proposal funded by five separate airlines in the United States. A prototype made test flights in 1938, but only United and American Airlines pushed development that led to the DC–4, which first flew in 1942.

The Douglas C–54, an unpressurized craft, was the largest transport mass produced during the war.

Lockheed's C–69 Constellation was pressurized for higher altitude where fewer weather problems and less atmospheric drag permitted faster speeds.

An unpressurized airliner, the C–54 military type appeared in many variants. Early models carried only twenty-six passengers, but the manufacturer quickly introduced stretched versions to carry between forty and eighty people. The C–54B, for example, typically seated fifty medical evacuees or twenty-six stretcher cases. The C–54A represented a heavy-lift type, equipped with an oversized cargo door and capable of loading fourteen thousand pounds or more, including vehicles like trucks and road-building equipment. Later versions of the C–54 carried more than twice the payload and could fly missions of more than forty-four hundred miles at a cruising speed of 220 mph; the airplane boasted a top speed of about 285 mph. Wartime production totaled 953 aircraft, the largest transport to be mass-produced during World War II. A number of executive modifications appeared, though none so well known as the "Sacred Cow," equipped for the personal use of President Franklin D. Roosevelt. Like the C–47, dozens of C–54 transports soldiered on into the postwar era at Air Force and allied bases on every continent.

Toward the end of the war, C–54 transports were joined by a different four-engine civil airliner equipped with tricycle landing gear and built by Lockheed. In its prewar development as the Lockheed Model 49, the Constellation emerged as a large pressurized aircraft, a feature that permitted flights at higher altitudes where there were fewer weather problems and where lower atmospheric drag conditions allowed for higher speeds. From the start, the Constellation represented outstanding performance, being capable of cruising at 300 mph, carrying more than thirty-two thousand

Igor Sikorsky was an aeronautical engineer who pioneered helicopter development in the 1930s.

This Sikorsky R–5A helicopter was stripped of all excess weight for use in rescue missions.

pounds of cargo, and transporting sixty-four passengers over intercontinental distances. Military versions of the C–69 saw limited service, with just twenty-two produced for the AAF and only a few available for operations by the end of the war. But the C–69 heralded the kind of speeds and operating altitudes that became commonplace after the war. Dozens of Constellation variants joined the service through the following years, remaining on active duty into the Vietnam War era in a variety of roles, including electronic surveillance and countermeasures.

Helicopters

The airlift experience in World War II also included the AAF's first operational deployment of helicopters. Brilliant Russian émigré Igor Sikorsky had studied rotary-wing aircraft in Imperial Russia before settling in the United States after the Russian Revolution of 1917–18. Following major success with large flying boats, Sikorsky returned to helicopter development in the 1930s. The historic flight of the Sikorsky VS–300 in 1939 is generally acknowledged to be the first use of modern, practical helicopter design. Military interest led to a production model, the Vought-Sikorsky R–4, introduced in 1942. Its 180-hp engine gave it a top speed of 75 mph and a range of 130 miles. The R–4 could lift only one passenger in addition to the pilot. The aircraft initially served as a coastal-patrol helicopter in the United States, entering service in 1943. The same year, several helicopters were sent to Burma to see how the unusual-looking vehicle would operate in hot, humid jungle environments. The AAF eventually received 132 models of this pioneer helicopter design.

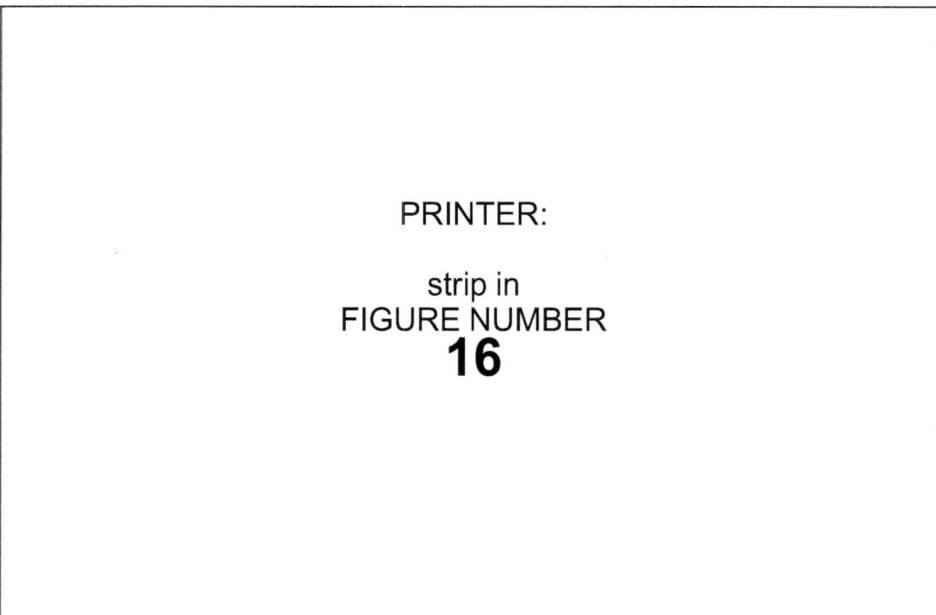

The R–4 helicopter carried the pilot and one passenger on coastal patrol duties.

Gliders

The role of glider pilots and glider troops is often overlooked. Sixty-five hundred glider pilots served in U.S. units, a unique group who not only commanded aircraft but also fought as infantry after landing their gliders. Glider pilots often became the first airborne troops to step onto enemy-held soil, and they played a key role in preliminary assaults from Sicily to northern Europe to the Far East. These pilots also experienced some of the highest casualty rates in World War II. Walter Cronkite, who became one of the most respected broadcast journalists of the postwar era, rode into combat in a glider when he was starting his career as a war correspondent in 1944. Cronkite later characterized his experience colorfully and succinctly: "It was a lifetime cure for constipation" (quoted in McAuliffe, June 1994).

Because parachute drops left troops dispersed over a comparatively broad area, the appeal of gliders lay in their ability to deliver larger numbers of soldiers into a smaller perimeter as a more cohesive fighting force. Also, gliders could carry some wheeled vehicles, mortars, and light artillery that could not be parachuted from World War II cargo transports. Essentially, the role of glider troops was to make landings ahead of the ground forces and take enemy strongholds by surprise. Key objectives included enemy artillery batteries, bridges, and choke points along rail or road lines. Still, glider troops carried limited supplies, relying on the main force to relieve them in short order. Glider pilots who survived rotated back to their bases for subsequent missions.

America's rush to develop gliders followed the stunning success of the German glider assault on the Belgian fortress of Eben Emael in May 1940. Using ten gliders holding only seventy-eight combat troops, the Germans landed within the fortress perimeter, placed demolition charges at strategic points, and disabled most of the Belgian guns and crews in the first few minutes of the assault. Some hours later, the Germans forced the surrender of the fort's 780-man garrison, at a cost to the glider troops of six dead and twenty wounded. In 1941, the German attack on the British-held island of Crete appeared to drive home the new reality of large-scale glider assaults. In fact, the Germans suffered crippling losses of glider troops, gliders, pilots, and tow airplanes, but both Britain and the United States continued to develop similar glider attack capability because it seemed so tactically effective.

The crash program to create production gliders finally settled on a design submitted by the Waco Aircraft Company of Troy, Ohio, well known for its series of high-performance private airplanes of the 1930s. Waco's CG–4A glider hardly resembled the nimble light airplanes that had made the firm's reputation. The glider had a boxy fuselage, a blunt nose, and shoulder-mounted wings supported by struts. The fixed gear was mounted directly to the fuselage and provided clearance of only two feet or so.

Gliders like this Waco CG–4A could transport land vehicles, light artillery, and troops.

Waco's design used a fabric-covered tubular steel frame, plywood flooring, and minimal instruments. Without flaps, the heavily loaded glider had an alarming sink rate; free flight at the end of a tether demanded constant attention; and landing amounted to a controlled crash. Normally, the CG–4A carried up to fifteen troops, including the pilot and copilot. With a total payload capacity of some 3,800 pounds, these gliders could transport items as large as a Jeep, a quarter-ton truck, or a 75-mm howitzer and its crew. It had a portside door, and the front end swung up on hinges to unload larger cargo. About 12,400 models of the CG–4A went to the AAF along with 940 more for British forces, who named it the Hadrian. Through a reverse Lend-Lease agreement, AAF units in Britain received some twenty-six hundred examples of the Airspeed MK–1 Horsa, a larger glider capable of carrying up to thirty combat troops or 7,120 pounds of cargo. Like the Waco, the Horsa also had a breakaway tail section and a large cargo door on the port side, just aft of the cockpit. The British craft used a wooden frame construction that tended to collapse and spray dangerous splinters on landing impact. Pilots and troops alike favored the CG–4A, although it had its own history of weaknesses.

The urgent need for gliders to use in training as well as for combat meant that production was farmed out to a variety of firms, many of which had little or no experience in aircraft construction. Ford Motor Company produced the largest share of CG–4A gliders—more than four thousand of them—but other suppliers reflected a disappointing cross-section of production know-how. Ford, along with Waco and Cessna, had prior experience, in contrast to Anheuser-Busch and the Gibson Refrigerator Company, two of the larger firms involved in final production. Over 115 other contractors participated, including companies like the Steinway Piano Company and the H. J. Heinz Pickle Company, which turned out wing spars and wing assemblies, respectively. Ongoing quality control problems came to a head in the summer of 1943. During an air show in

Saint Louis, Missouri, the mayor and several other city officials, including a pair of high-ranking Air Force officers, climbed into a newly delivered CG–4A for a demonstration flight. Just after takeoff, one wing snapped off, sending the stricken glider into a nose dive that killed the crew and all passengers. An inquiry cited faulty workmanship for a wing-root attachment, and this led to stringent new quality controls.

The CG–4A gliders were towed by C–47 transports at speeds less than 120 mph and had a stalling speed of about 44 mph. They were not always reliable even under tow, during which the glider pilot had constantly to keep his craft's tether aligned within a few degrees of the tow plane. His diligence produced a cone of safe tethered flight for both the tower and towee called, appropriately, "the angle of the dangle." If caught fully loaded in turbulent conditions, gliders were known to disintegrate, spilling their cargoes or hapless troops to the ground far below. One surviving glider pilot remembered a harrowing landing in Germany when a phosphorous shell set a fabric-covered wing afire. As he descended through haze into the battle zone, he suddenly saw power lines directly ahead, but was able to fly his glider underneath them and complete a safe landing.

Collectively, these transports and gliders represented the heart of the AAF and Allied airlift and airborne assault forces. That they performed effectively in every theater, under the harshest environments of arctic cold and desert or tropical heat, attested to their sturdy design and perhaps even more to the efforts of the aircrews and ground personnel who kept them flying. The transports and pilots of the ATC not only supported the Army Air Forces wherever needed, but also became the official carriers for the entire War Department. With the development of routes throughout the central and southern Pacific, the ATC had become a worldwide network of awesome capability by 1945.

In addition to the special flying boats and Boeing transports acquired at the war's outbreak, the principal ATC transports included workhorses such as the C–46, C–47, C–54, and C–87. On a global basis, these aircraft carried out a wide array of assignments. Pan Am's Clippers took President Roosevelt across the South Atlantic to various wartime conferences with Churchill, Stalin, and others, just as different airplanes flew dignitaries and high-ranking officers to additional meetings on every continent. Over the course of the war years, the ATC carried just about anything that could be loaded aboard its aircraft. Indeed, as described in the official history, *The Army Air Forces in World War II,* ATC aircraft airlifted everything "from bulldozers to blood plasma, from college professors to Hollywood entertainers, from high-explosive ammunition to the most delicate signal equipment, from eminent scientists to the most obscure technician, from heads of state to the ordinary G.I." On return trips, the airplanes carried strategic cargoes such as tungsten from China, cobalt from Africa, and quinine from Latin America. And from every war zone came planeloads of wounded G.I.s grateful for such rapid return to modern medical wards in the United States.

When ATC was established in June 1942, the number of its personnel stood at 11,000; this number had risen to 125,000 by July 1944. The ATC aircraft fleet had reached 1,000 by the end of 1943 and surpassed 3,000 barely a year later. By July 1945, ATC transports were carrying 275,000 passengers per month, crisscrossing the globe with the regularity of passenger trains. At the same time, the ATC's Ferrying Division continued to fly combat airplanes to military bases at home and abroad, delivering 30,000 in 1942, 72,000 in 1943, and 108,000 in 1944. Prior to V-J Day in August 1945, the ATC had already delivered 57,000 additional aircraft to combat units.

AIRBORNE OPERATIONS IN THE MEDITERRANEAN

When the Allies first began plans in early 1942 for the invasion of North Africa, they made no assignments for airborne troops. Eventually, the need to ensure air superiority over the invasion beaches became a priority, leading to a decision to insert paratroops at two airfields in western Algeria. The task went to troopers of the 2d Battalion, 503d Parachute Infantry. The mission required a fifteen hundred-mile flight from England to North Africa—the longest continuous sortie by any airborne forces in World War II.

Haste in planning the operation exposed a number of serious problems in its execution. Many of the C–47 pilots were recent recruits from commercial airlines, unfamiliar with the geography of the mission and also untrained in the niceties of flying in formation during the night. Many navigators arrived to join crews only a few days before the mission's scheduled departure. Thirty-nine airplanes left their English bases after nightfall on November 7. Despite the unfamiliar strain of formation flying at night and through fog, thirty-two of the transports still held a ragged position in the formation at sunrise. One diverted to Gibraltar because of engine trouble, and several others delivered their troops to French and Spanish Morocco, where they were interned. The remaining transports arrived over the target area, where most elected to land in a dry lake bed miles away from the airfield objectives, and the remaining paratroops jumped into terrain between the two airfields, leaving them in a poor tactical position. U.S. motorized units arrived at the airfields before any paratroopers had advanced to their objectives. All in all, the first real combat exercise for U.S. paratroopers did not transpire as intended.

During September 1943, U.S. Army and Air Force officers discussed different plans for airborne operations at Salerno, on Italy's western coast, as well as possible air landings at Rome. Despite some detailed planning

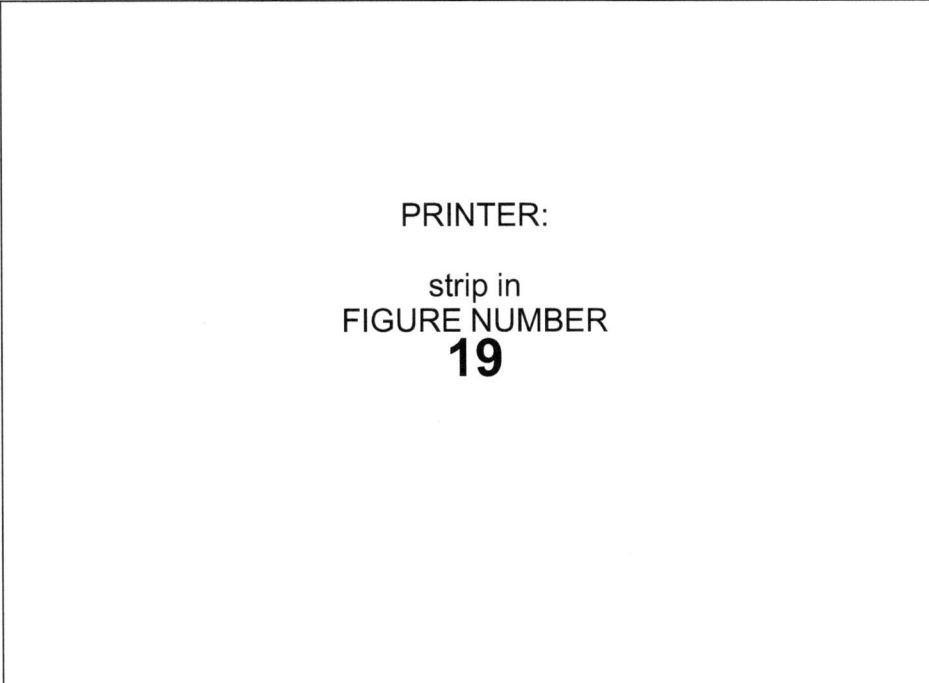

Paratroopers prepare their packs and parachutes before boarding a C–47 for jumps in Sicily in July 1944.

for several possibilities, nothing materialized because of the serious logistical problems in reinforcing airborne troops far behind enemy lines and the inability of Italian authorities to guarantee assistance for landing at Italian airfields near Rome, where German forces remained strong.

Eventually, an emergency request from Gen. Mark Clark, who needed reinforcements after the Salerno landings, led to action. Over successive nights, AAF transports dropped two infantry regiments and two engineering companies at Paestum, a coastal town south of Salerno. Brig. Gen. James M. Gavin, who led this mission, felt that the sudden presence of U.S. troops, far from where the Germans expected them, played a key role in stabilizing the right flank of Clark's offensive. The second operation, at the mountain town of Avellino, a motor-road hub twenty miles north of the Salerno beaches, did not go nearly as well. A total of 640 troopers jumped, and about 500 eventually reached Allied lines. High mountains surrounding the town made it difficult to spot, and only a few pilots identified the proper drop zone. The troops became scattered over one hundred square miles. Gavin stated that "it is doubtful that [the operation] had any decisive bearing on the outcome of the Battle of Salerno." The isolated paratroopers proved no more than a military nuisance to German commanders.

By the summer of 1944, after nearly two years of training and combat experience in North Africa, American strategists approached airborne operations much more confidently. For example, for the invasion of Sicily in July 1943, U.S. commanders assigned a reinforced 505th Parachute Infantry of the 82d Airborne Division. Their objective was the high ground inland from the invasion beaches where Allied occupation would insulate the southwestern Sicilian coast from enemy counterattack. A British airborne brigade planned a glider attack behind the southeastern coast in order to capture a crucial bridge, the Ponte Grande near Syracuse, and to knock out coastal batteries facing the British invasion sector.

For each of the Allied units, confidence was misplaced. The British force of 144 tow airplanes with gliders ran into gale-force winds that scattered the units. Only twelve gliders finally landed near their objectives; amidst confusion about their release point, nearly half the glider force was cut free too soon and crash-landed in the sea, drowning some 250 soldiers. The survivors somehow managed to neutralize the coastal battery and aided friendly ground forces in taking the bridge. The U.S. paratroop forces were also scattered by similar gale-force winds, and transport pilots became confused as haze, dust, and smoke from the preliminary bombardment obscured vital checkpoints. Airplanes arrived over Sicily from every direction, and 4,440 paratroopers who made the jump were scattered across the countryside. In small groups, the troopers made their way toward the sound of artillery fire along the invasion beaches and actually helped divert an Italian counterattack until advancing U.S. troops arrived. On the second day, officers decided to send in 2,000 paratroopers as reinforcements, timing the mission shortly after midnight. Despite warnings to Allied shipping and antiaircraft batteries now ashore, nervous gunners opened fire on the low-flying C–47s. They shot down two dozen airplanes, three dozen more received heavy damage, and an estimated two hundred casualties resulted from the confusion.

In the process of conducting these missions, the AAF had learned harsh lessons about preliminary planning, logistics, and launching reasonably large formations of paratroop-laden transport aircraft. The service had yet to come to terms with the realities of chaotic events such as adverse winds and poor visibility over target areas, to say nothing of trigger-happy Allied gun crews. Still, paratroopers on the ground maintained an admirable level of fighting spirit and demonstrated an ability to recover and assault their objective. Such lessons could be applied to much larger and more intricate offensives in the Mediterranean and western Europe, backed by greater numbers of transports and more experienced pilots and staff officers.

The hard experiences of Africa, Italy, and Sicily definitely held a cumulative value. Hundreds of small technical problems had been resolved. A core of officers acquired invaluable experience in planning airborne assaults and arranging appropriate logistical support for parachute troops on the ground. Uncertainties about how to use airborne troops gave way to realistic doctrine. "Clearly," Gavin wrote later, "they must be employed in mass and not in small packets." Moving from formations of a few dozen transports, Gavin and his cohorts were now ready to undertake actions requiring hundreds of aircraft and tens of thousands of troops. The next phase of airborne operations lay in western Europe.

SPECIAL MISSIONS

FRANTIC

Meanwhile, within the framework of ATC requirements and airborne assault campaigns, a variety of special operations took place. One of these proceeded under the code name, FRANTIC. During the winter of 1943–44, as Germany moved many factories to the east and out of range of Allied bomber strikes, the concept of "shuttle bombing" took hold. The idea rested on bombing missions that could originate in Britain and at Allied bases in Italy, strike German targets at long range, and then proceed to convenient airfields in the Soviet Union. Refueled and armed, the bombers would hit German targets again on their way home. After several frustrating planning sessions, Soviet Premier Joseph Stalin finally agreed to the concept in February 1944.

In haste, the U.S. Strategic Air Forces in Europe set up an Eastern Command to carry out the shuttle-bomb requirements for FRANTIC. Heavy equipment and bulky supplies went by sea to the port of Archangel, north of Leningrad (Saint Petersburg), and then to a quartet of new airfields in the Ukraine. Additional supplies and key personnel would fly in on ATC airplanes from U.S. bases in Iran. Delicate negotiations finally fixed a total of forty-two round-trip ATC missions to make the bases operational for the AAF, and allowed an additional rate of two weekly support missions to sustain the U.S. contingent. The issue of flight communications eventually ended with a compromise, allowing U.S. crews to carry out navigation and radio duties with a Soviet observer resident at all related communications centers.

Eventually, the ATC in support of FRANTIC delivered some 450 personnel and thirty-six thousand pounds of cargo by June 1944. The same month, Gen. Ira Eaker made the first shuttle bombing mission with 129 B–17 bombers of the Mediterranean Air Force. Operations continued through the middle of August 1944, by which time the original sixteen targets identified for Operation FRANTIC had been taken by the rapidly advancing Soviet offensives. A reluctant Stalin agreed to a winter intermission of operations; U.S. and Soviet advances by the spring of 1945 ended the need for shuttle missions and the ATC flew out the last U.S. contingent in June 1945. Operation FRANTIC demonstrated the flexibility of airlift equipment and personnel. It also demonstrated the political role of airlift logistics in terms of operational support that would have been impossible by conventional ground-based means.

CARPETBAGGER *and the Balkans*

Other special airlift operations involved a cloak-and-dagger environment, inserting and extracting agents behind enemy lines, as well as supplying resistance forces throughout Europe and the Balkans. Such was the purpose of Operation CARPETBAGGER, launched in the spring of 1944. Special elements of the Eighth Air Force used a variety of equipment, including some forty models of the B–24, modified for clandestine missions over enemy territory. The ubiquitous C–47 transports also played a major role. All of these aircraft and crews were especially busy during 1944, supplying insurgent groups in France and northern Europe during the preparations for the Normandy invasion and during the subsequent Allied advance out of the Normandy beachhead. During that year alone, CARPETBAGGER sorties numbered 1,860 and accounted for some 1,000 personnel drop-and-recovery missions, plus delivery of more than 20,000 containers and 111,000 packages. Other activities included more than 2,000 sorties to drop propaganda leaflets, as well as missions to broadcast Allied radio messages or to jam enemy radio programs.

Although virtually every special operation was judged vital, some especially important missions were flown to the Balkans. Numbers of AAF flight crews and Allied personnel were evacuated by air from remote airstrips. One extended series of covert missions launched from Italy during 1944–45 airlifted more than two thousand partisans from positions behind enemy lines. Using rough, clandestine landing strips, C–47 transports made 50 percent of the necessary sorties. In another case in early 1944, a trio of C–47s towed three Waco gliders loaded with British and Soviet personnel who landed the gliders inside Yugoslavia.

THE ASSAULT ON EUROPE

OVERLORD

The huge and complex Allied invasion of Normandy on June 6, 1944, known as Operation OVERLORD, included crucial operations of airborne troops. The Ninth Air Force included the IX Troop Carrier Command, the unit given the job of carrying the U.S. 82d and 101st Airborne Divisions into combat. In the days prior to the invasion, the AAF collected over nine hundred aircraft, mostly C–47 transports, plus some one hundred gliders. Their objective was to secure the southern flank of the Normandy beach invasion sector. Loaded during the night of June 5–6, thirteen thousand U.S. paratroopers began their flight across the English Channel, scheduled to reach six drop zones during the early morning hours and under cover of darkness. At the same time, several thousand British airborne troops departed for additional drop zones along the northern flank of the Normandy landing areas.

The initial wave of U.S. transports crossed the coast in good shape, although their arrival alerted German gunners and heavy antiaircraft fire affected all the transports that followed. Additionally, a shift in weather patterns generated clouds, fog, and adverse winds. Formations began to drift and break up; confusion mounted in the darkness as dozens of airplanes lost contact with their original formations. Analysts later concluded that only 10 percent of the U.S. airborne forces hit their drop zones; some 50 percent of the troops parachuted one or two miles away from their intended zones. Confused and disoriented, they wasted many hours trying to find their own units, often straggling along with whatever U.S. paratroops they found. The confusion in the darkness was compounded by the towering hedgerows of the Normandy region. The hedgerows, impenetrable tangles of bushes and undergrowth, lined roads and fields at a height of five to twelve feet, making cross-country sighting and travel difficult even in daylight.

There was one advantage in all this. For the Germans, with reports of enemy paratroopers cascading in from all points of the compass, organizing a logical, effective counterattack against the airborne forces proved temporarily daunting. This gave U.S. troops some additional time to try to lash together effective combat units, but the general dispersion undermined a central tenet of airborne operations of keeping their modest forces concentrated in one area. Of the sixty-six hundred men in the 101st Airborne Division, only one-third were under a central command at the end of the day.

The night operations also affected glider missions. The temperamental gliders, in the hands of comparatively inexperienced pilots, were tricky to land in daylight on a calm day. Bringing them down safely at night, in extremely poor visibility and on a hedgerow-carpeted terrain, appeared unusually foolhardy. But senior officers in the Allied planning committees insisted on it, citing potentially extreme casualties from German antiaircraft fire during daylight. Despite bitter objections from officers in airborne squadrons, planners held to their decision to land the gliders at night.

The Normandy landings involved several hundred CG–4A types and British Horsa gliders. Invasion timetables called for glider assaults in the predawn hours of D-Day, about five hours before the main force of troops hit the beaches. The total complement of glider and airborne troops came to three full airborne divisions, and their objectives involved occupying key areas at either end of the Normandy beachhead as well as

Douglas C–47s towed gliders to the Normandy coast on June 6, 1944.

holding important bridges and roads to choke off early counterattacks. All glider pilots received intensive briefings about their landing zones in order to minimize confusion in identifying assigned objectives. When there was light enough to see, this procedure worked well. As one glider pilot recalled later, he felt as though he were driving to his own farm; coming in for his landing, he recognized trees, fences, and houses. Nonetheless, intelligence misled a number of pilots, who found that twenty-foot-high trees marked on briefing charts turned out to be eighty feet high. Pilots were also told to use hedgerows as a pliant barrier to slow them down on landing, only to find that hedgerows were generally unyielding and often covered stone walls. The dangers in landing included "Rommel's asparagus," long rows of twelve-foot posts, many wired to mines, placed to rip apart gliders steering for apparently usable landing zones.

In retrospect, the OVERLORD experience underscored the usefulness of airborne troops and the possibilities of aerial resupply. Nonetheless, many officers became discouraged about mounting nighttime operations, and airborne assaults held little chance of success unless favorable weather held and air superiority remained inviolate.

MARKET-GARDEN

Following the retreat of German units into Holland and southern Germany, the Allied commanders pondered their next moves. Field Marshal Sir Bernard L. Montgomery argued for a bold push to outflank German forces along the northern battle line by airlifting three airborne divisions for attacks deep behind the enemy's main position. By this time, Gen. Dwight D. Eisenhower had assumed command of all Allied ground forces on the European continent, and Montgomery had to win Eisenhower's support for this daring operation. Montgomery's gambit required the airborne units to open and hold a corridor sixty-five miles long, running from Holland's southern border to the city of Arnhem on the Rhine River. With this narrow passage cleared of German troops, Montgomery proposed to launch the British Second Army on a headlong rush up the corridor, across the Rhine, and into the heartland of Germany. But to cross the Rhine, the airborne units had to make sure they took the Arnhem bridge intact, as well as several others along the corridor at Eindhoven and Nijmegen. Therefore, it was essential to put the Allied units down close to their assigned bridgeheads and to keep them supplied by air until relieved by the British Second Army as it advanced. Given the success of the Allied advance to date, the mounting logistical assets from the Channel inland, and control of the air, Montgomery eventually secured Eisenhower's agreement. If successful, the action could end the war in Europe within weeks. Operation MARKET-GARDEN was set for September 1944.

Mission planners envisioned a three-day operation to airlift a total of thirty-five thousand troops plus support equipment from England; more than twenty thousand men were to be inserted the first day alone, along with five hundred vehicles, 330 artillery pieces, and 590 tons of other equipment. On the day of the offensive, some two thousand troop airplanes and six hundred gliders would take to the air, along with two thousand more airplanes—fighters and bombers—to fly top cover and to hit German positions in the attack area.

The architects of MARKET-GARDEN knew it held high risks. Experience showed that the effectiveness of airborne troops slipped rapidly the longer they had to hold their isolated objectives. Moreover, their firepower invariably amounted to less than that of their adversaries, especially if the defenders could introduce heavy armor into the battle. Inserting paratroops and glider forces sixty-five miles into German territory seemed almost foolhardy. But Eisenhower and Montgomery accepted intelligence reports that most German forces in the landing zones were inexperienced garrison troops and other units pulled out of action elsewhere because they had been decimated.

The components of the First Allied Airborne Army, commanded by U.S. Lt. Gen. Lewis Brereton, were battle-hardened troops who were superbly equipped, rested, at full strength, and eager to tangle with the enemy. Units of the U.S. 82d and 101st Airborne Divisions had fought at Normandy; the British 1 Airborne Division had fought through Sicily and Italy. The 101st, under Brig. Gen. Maxwell Taylor, had the task of landing near Eindhoven to take the city and its key bridges. Brig. Gen. James Gavin's 82d had similar objectives at Grave and Nijmegen. The most distant target, the bridge over the Lower Rhine and Arnhem, went to British forces under Major General Robert Urquhart, including the British 1 Airborne and a Polish brigade. The overall tactical commander, the British general, Frederick Browning, recognized the risks, particularly for the British 1 Airborne. Browning, the husband of novelist Daphne du Maurier, also made a prophetic remark. Told that he needed to hold out at Arnhem for at least two days, Browning said that the contingent there could probably control its position for four. "But," he observed, "I think we might be going a bridge too far" (Sears, 1991, pp. 215–16).

On September 17, 1944, Operation MARKET-GARDEN got under way. The first reports looked encouraging, as early airdrops put the U.S. units into their assigned target areas. But the timetable began to unravel at the British end, as airborne artillery and equipment often went down wide of their marks. Bad weather and quickly mobilized German defenders took a heavy toll, especially on the British. Parachutists and glider troops went into action without the margins of fire support and supplies planned for them. Several critical bridges remained in German hands. When the sun set three days later, Montgomery's Second Army had failed to advance and tenacious Allied airborne forces held only a narrow strip of territory that ran thirty-five miles between Eindhoven and Nijmegen. Strong German resistance elsewhere had brought the Second Army to a standstill in its attempt to relieve British airborne forces at Arnhem. Although Montgomery felt encouraged that the Arnhem bridge remained in British hands, the battalion of British troops at one end of it had been cut off and encircled by much stronger German forces. Two more days of aerial resupply efforts around Arnhem led to the loss of twenty-three transports, and only a fraction of several hundred tons of supplies had fallen into Allied positions. Another operation, an attempt to drop fifteen hundred troop reinforcements from a Polish parachute brigade, was frustrated by strong gusts that prevented one-third of the Poles from jumping and carried most of the rest onto the wrong bank of the Rhine, where they suffered heavy losses. Airdrops of more than three thousand reinforcements and supplies to American forces were marginally better because the two U.S. airborne divisions had gained control of a larger area.

At the end of a week of agonizing debate and failed relief efforts, Montgomery ordered withdrawal of all units south of the Rhine and closed the gate on Operation MARKET-GARDEN. Overall, a postaction analysis left little to feel good about. Of 35,000 troops committed by the Allies, 11,583 became casualties and, of those, 9,333 were listed as killed or missing. Of the huge flotilla of transports, air commanders reported 1,265 damaged aircraft and another 153 destroyed. In addition, Allied air forces wrote off eighty-seven fighters and bombers. The nine days of operational effort had been bedeviled by bad weather, a major factor in the disappointing efforts at reinforcement and resupply.

Allied air operations had accomplished little interdiction of enemy transport and communications. Military intelligence had clearly underestimated German military capabilities and even failed to locate and identify major threats, like a Panzer division in the area. Allied efforts to coordinate communications and supply revealed significant gaps. MARKET-GARDEN was a promising and audacious concept, launched with commendable expertise in marshaling a large force of transports, gliders, and

C–46s are readied to carry paratroopers to Operation VARSITY in the industrial city of Wesel, Germany.

troops. Loading, transporting, and delivering so many airplanes and troops onto enemy territory was no mean logistical feat. But contingency planning to cope with the vagaries of weather and unanticipated enemy resistance proved fallible, and a heroic effort was, in the end, undone.

Bastogne and VARSITY

Despite the bitter experience of MARKET-GARDEN, gliders successfully relieved troops cut off in enemy territory on more than one occasion. During late December 1944, Brig. Gen. Anthony C. McAuliffe commanded soldiers surrounded at Bastogne, Belgium, during the Battle of the Bulge. McAuliffe achieved immortality for his defiant "Nuts!" in response to German demands for his surrender. Meanwhile, McAuliffe's battered command included five hundred badly wounded men; gas, ammunition, and rations continued to dwindle as it became questionable whether General Patton's relief forces could break through in time. While Patton's advance remained hours away, U.S. glider pilots launched a rescue mission through intense German ground fire and flak to deliver supplies and medical teams to keep the Bastogne forces in the fight. Subsequent parachute drops supplied the troops around Bastogne until relief columns finally arrived.

One more large paratroop operation remained—Operation VARSITY, directed at Wesel, an industrial city on the Rhine at the mouth of the Lippe River. Field Marshal Montgomery's main forces planned to cross the Rhine nearby, so the Wesel area's bridges and transport network represented a key military objective. But before Montgomery's extensive planning and labored execution took place in the north, units of advancing U.S. forces to the south already had taken the bridge at Remagen and forced their way across the Rhine at other points. Operation VARSITY was later much criticized as an unnecessary operation. Even so, its conduct demonstrated a level of maturity in the planning and execution of airborne warfare.

The 17th Airborne Division, representing the U.S. contingent, now boasted greater strengths in parachute platoons as well as glider companies. Planners inserted a third battalion for the glider company regiment. There was increased firepower throughout, including glider battalions that landed with Jeeps and 105-mm howitzers, and other units equipped with new weapons like 57-mm and 75-mm recoilless rifles. The latter helped resolve a significant problem in the ability of airborne units to deal with enemy armor. Troop transports and glider pilots planned operations from a considerable reservoir of large-action experience in the western European arena. Based on accumulated operational confidence, many tow airplanes pulled two gliders in their wake. Troop Carrier Command employed a new version of the C–46 Commando, equipped with doors on each side of its fuselage, a feature that allowed paratroopers to jump simultaneously from both sides of the aircraft. The opportunity to unload parachute troops over enemy territory in one-half the usual time for each transport enhanced survival of the airplane and also enhanced the concentration of troops on landing. A number of factors influenced the decision to jump during daylight, but the bitter memories of MARKET-GARDEN clearly played a role in the final plan to launch a nighttime river crossing followed by the airborne assault not long after sunrise.

VARSITY's aerial action began during the morning of March 24, 1945. Covered by some eight hundred fighters, 1,696 transports and 1,348 gliders flew over the landing zone, a long line of aircraft that took two and one-half hours to complete their paratroop drops and glider deliveries. During the day, another two thousand fighters provided air cover for resupply sorties that included 240 Liberators which dropped more than 580 tons of supplies. The initial glider landings provided assault troops with 695 vehicles and 113 pieces of artillery. Despite fierce resistance from some German units and comparatively high casualty rates among the attacking Allied forces, most objectives were taken within a few hours. By nightfall, British ground troops had made contact with the airborne forces and the attack on Wesel had succeeded.

Forty-four transports and fifteen Liberators were destroyed in VARSITY operations, attempting to resupply the airborne troops. The 17th Airborne lost 159 men with 522 wounded; the British 6 Airborne listed 347 dead and 731 wounded. By comparison, two U.S. infantry divisions that crossed the Rhine in the same operation had 44 dead and 450 wounded. Airborne assaults remained highly vulnerable to effectively directed enemy fire. At the same time, the sight of so many airplanes in the air and the effective concentration of airborne forces in a visibly successful attack against an entrenched enemy position generated great enthusiasm from Allied observers. Taking place beyond the Rhine, along with additional

Allied thrusts across the river, Operation VARSITY underscored the accelerating collapse of Nazi Germany and a rising confidence in victory for the Allies in western Europe.

FLYING THE HUMP

In the process of conducting the postwar analysis of air operations, authors of the *United States Strategic Bombing Survey* paid attention to the story of airlift activities. In its study of the China-Burma-India theater, the survey attached particular value to the airlift factor and the role of the ATC. "The major significance, for the future, of all air operation in CBI was the development of air transport operations," the survey concluded. The airlift's success was all the more notable because of its hurried deployment and the formidable geographic region in which it operated. As the survey observed, "the terrain of Burma and China and the absence of land lines of communication forced all agencies in the theater to turn to the airplane—initially as an afterthought and an emergency last-chance measure." The flexibility of air transportation offered planners a unique tool "to meet the exigencies of the various situations." Summing up, the survey declared that "air transport operations expanded beyond the wildest predictions of 1942—expanded because it was the one agency which could succeed."

Regarding the CBI theater, the military situation in 1942 appeared to be highly unfavorable. The Imperial Japanese Army presence in China to-

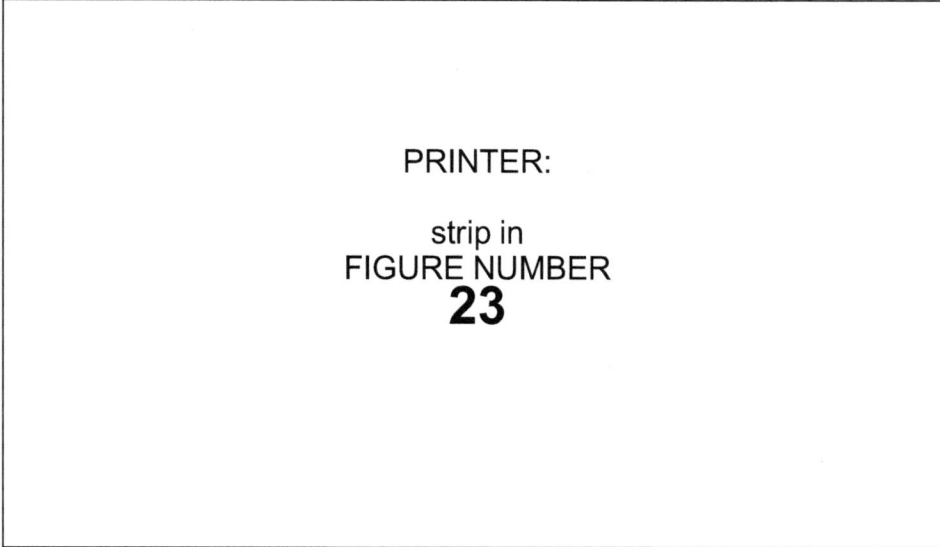

The H–6 helicopter, able to land in clearings as small as 65 feet across, evacuated wounded from jungles in the China-Burma-India theater.

taled one million troops. The Chinese forces opposing them numbered in the hundreds of thousands, but were critically disadvantaged by their tenuous supply line stretching hundreds of miles to the west in India. Moreover, this line to Allied support snaked through impenetrable jungles and towering mountain passes of the Himalayas. The mountains, rising to twenty thousand feet and more, presented a seemingly impossible operational challenge. With the cynical cockiness typical of soldiers and airmen, troops in the region reduced the Himalayas by way of semantics, simply referring to them as "The Hump."

Following the invasion of China in 1937, Japanese forces succeeded in occupying or controlling virtually all of China's Pacific coast and large parts of the interior; the Japanese navy commanded all ocean approaches. In the spring of 1942, Japanese units overran Burma, on India's northern border, cutting off the last significant land routes that supplied the struggling armies of Generalissimo Chiang Kai-Shek in China. The United States and its allies needed to keep China in the war because its forces preoccupied hundreds of thousands of Japanese troops. This holding action would permit the Allies to attack Axis powers in the European and Mediterranean theaters, at the same time building the necessary logistical infrastructure to challenge and defeat Japan in the Far East. But for this grand strategy to work, China had to be supplied. The loss of Burma and of its supply lines to China precipitated an emergency situation.

General Arnold had been worrying about the fragile supply lines to China even before the loss of Burma. During the 1930s, the China National Aviation Corporation (CNAC) had pioneered air routes over the Himalayas. CNAC operated with the support of the Chinese government and the expertise of Pan American Airways. With Arnold's support, CNAC became a contractor to operate air cargo services between India and China, although it was clear that far more capacity was needed. Accordingly, the Tenth Air Force, based in India, took responsibility for substantial air cargo flights and began operations over the Hump in April 1942. In two months, the Tenth Air Force carried 196 tons of cargo, and CNAC delivered 112 tons. Summer monsoons nearly terminated flights, but the two units were delivering one thousand tons a month by the end of the year. This, however, was far short of the ten thousand tons required by the Chinese each month. A drastic reorganization ensued.

Staff reports analyzing early failures pointed to a variety of problems, including shortages in aircraft and crews. Poor maintenance kept many airplanes grounded. Operational missions dealt with foul weather, flight at high altitudes, and spoiling forays by Japanese fighter airplanes. Moreover, Tenth Air Force commanders did not seem committed to an all-out effort to sustain Hump operations. In October 1942, Arnold decided to put the ATC in command of all Hump operations, and Tenth Air Force units on Hump assignments were transferred to the ATC in December. The ATC, with authority to handle all airlift requirements in the theater of operations, brought its special experience to sort out the problems in air transportation and cargo flying.

Heavily loaded transports began their runs to China after lifting off from hot, muggy airfields in India's eastern jungles, then struggled upward for altitude to clear the towering Himalayas. A direct route to Kunming, China, took four hours, at an average altitude of about sixteen thousand feet, and placed aircraft over areas within range of Japanese fighters. The ATC crews characteristically flew a dogleg to the north to escape enemy airplanes, even though the path stretched fuel reserves to the limit and required an operational altitude of twenty thousand feet to clear most of the Himalayan peaks. Many fliers wound up threading their way through available mountain passes at sixteen thousand feet, with snow-covered ridges and pinnacles rising on either side of them. In addition to the changeable weather high over the Himalayas, pilots flew across virtually impenetrable jungles on both sides of the menacing mountain ranges.

Over the Indian jungles, in particular, fliers had to contend with monsoon rainstorms for six months of every year. Landing strips and runways became muddy quagmires; fliers and ground personnel existed in a swampy world of sodden bunks, clothes, and tents. The C-46 Commandos mounted a many-paned windscreen and, when airborne, pilots discovered that the monsoons forced water through myriad gaps around the cockpit windows and left them as miserably soggy in the air as they were on the ground. Sheets of driving rain and turbulence around airfields often kept operations shut down for days at a time. Early in the war, the Japanese never expected Allied airlifts to work because of the mountains and the tropical storms, but the pressure to deliver needed war matériel often meant flying in conditions that normally kept airplanes on the ground. Veteran pilots explained the "CBI takeoff" to newcomers—if you could see the end of the runway through the rain and mist, then a takeoff was expected. At night, ATC crews sent a Jeep cruising ahead down the runway to clear it of cows, nocturnal animals, and curious natives.

Operational efficiency began to improve with the allocation of more airplanes and personnel, better weather forecasting, accumulated flight experience, and additional airfields where more attention was paid to drainage and weather resistance. The big push came in the wake of high-level Allied conferences during the spring of 1943. These meetings established a timetable for major European offensives and also resulted in agreements to accelerate the offensive against Japanese forces in Asia. A major key to this last objective involved a more prominent role for the ATC. President Roosevelt himself underscored a goal of ten thousand tons a month for the airlift into China, where political considerations implied heavier support of Chiang Kai-Shek's forces.

With this factor in mind, military planners shifted workers and equipment from road construction to building airfields. By the spring of 1945, a determined effort resulted in a total of thirteen primary bases for the

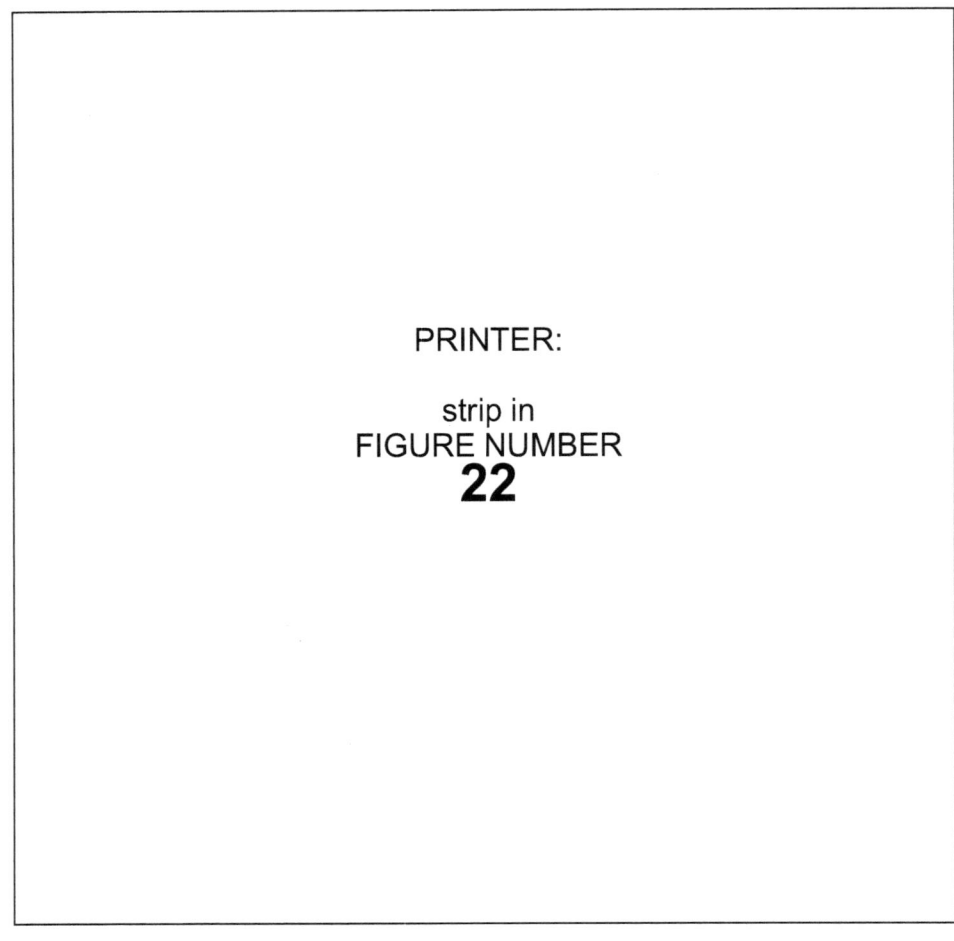

The window assembly on the C–46 had several panes—a configuration that yielded excellent visibility but failed to keep out monsoon rains.

ATC in India and six in China. Although ATC transports carried some equipment across the Hump to Chinese construction sites, the major factor on both sides of the Himalayas involved tens of thousands of local workers. The labor force—men, women, and children—carried out grueling tasks almost entirely by hand. Ox carts delivered rocks; a host of workers with crude picks reduced them to usable stone chips; hundreds more scooped them barehanded into baskets of woven vines, then hand-carried their burdens to the landing strip under construction. The stones were compacted by primitive boulder-filled rollers pulled along by gangs of straining laborers. News photographers recorded the throngs of workers—some one hundred thousand people—who swarmed back and forth to complete a six thousand-foot runway near the Yangtze River in China.

Still, nobody could reduce the Himalayas in size; banish the monsoon season; make the rough, rocky airstrips any smoother; bring down temperatures at sweltering Indian air bases; resolve the persistent shortages of personal supplies; or rectify the dozens of other major and minor complaints that affected morale. Despite such problems, ATC crews and personnel found ways to pursue specific goals and to gauge their achievements. As one observer said, they were "living like dogs and flying like fiends" (Spencer, 1992). Pilots and ground crews competed against others to see who could load the most cargo and complete the most missions. These contests soon embraced entire units and expanded to include categories such as fewest accidents and highest number of flying hours to an aircraft.

With gritty determination, the ATC pushed toward the goal of ten thousand tons of cargo a month. The target was not reached until the end of 1943, and came at the cost of many airplanes and aircrews. Many fliers simply lacked the experience for night flying or for operating the heavily loaded transports in hot weather and at high altitudes. Exhaustion of the pilots remained a constant factor. During the last half of 1943, some 150 major aircraft accidents resulted in more than 160 aircrew fatalities. Improved statistics for 1944 reflected rising operational experience, along with additional airplanes and pilots to enhance the frequency of flights. Monthly cargo deliveries climbed to fifteen thousand tons by the spring of 1944, and rose to more than thirty-four thousand tons by year's end.

Along the way, several administrative changes occurred. Brig. Gen. William H. Tunner took over Hump operations during the summer of 1944. Aircrews had dramatically raised the tonnage and frequency of flights, encouraged by Tunner's predecessor, Brig. Gen. Thomas Hardin. But there were still too many accidents, and morale remained dismally low. Tunner's prior success in running the huge and complex Ferrying Division of the ATC led the AAF to tap him as the man to improve delivery rates even further.

Tunner insisted on appropriate military dress and appearance, markedly improved meals and recreation opportunities for service members, instituted better weather forecasting, and streamlined maintenance procedures. Though some may have groused about these changes and the increased military protocol, Tunner had good reason for the new regulations. Shortly after arriving to take up his new duties in India, Tunner personally flew a C–46 over the Hump to China and back. During takeoff, he saw numerous scorched areas beside the runway—grim reminders of too many transports that had crashed and gone up in flames. His round-trip over the Himalayas brought home the exigencies of flying in bad weather and the vast, menacing threat to missions over such mountainous and broken terrain. His subsequent actions were all geared to reduce the accident rate and raise morale. Tunner was not above creative demonstrations to push his requests for additional resources back home, at one point making sure that reporters watched an elephant used to load crates into an ATC airplane in India.

By the end of World War II, Tunner's ATC Division had grown from 369 to 722 aircraft, and the number of personnel had swelled from twenty-six thousand to more than eighty-four thousand. Accelerated flight activity during the final offensives against Japanese forces in China meant one ATC transport took off every three minutes. Early in 1945, the monthly cargo delivered to China reached forty-four thousand tons, and it peaked at seventy-one thousand tons in July. Meanwhile, accident rates dropped by more than 50 percent.

The record of ATC achievements in the CBI theater unquestionably demonstrated the potential of major airlifts in modern warfare. Of all the supplies delivered to China from 1942 through 1945, 81 percent came by air over the Hump. Chinese forces tying up one million Japanese troops meant that the Japanese Imperial Army had far fewer resources to oppose the amphibious landings and other island campaigns mounted by America and its allies in the fighting throughout the Pacific. Airlift thus emerged as a significant new military consideration in future applications of air power.

OTHER FAR EAST MISSIONS

Operations involving airborne combat troops in the Pacific occurred toward the end of the war and were not as large or as widely reported as similar actions in the European theater. An exception included some of the most colorful airborne troop units and officers who served in the CBI theater.

Operation THURSDAY, which took place March 5–11, 1944, had the goals of dislodging the Japanese from Burma and reopening a long section of the Ledo Road to make it possible to resupply China overland from the Burmese town of Myitkyina. One British officer, Maj. Gen. Orde Wingate, had already become legendary for mounting successful guerrilla operations behind Japanese lines. An equally colorful American officer, Col. Philip Cochran, commanded the First Air Commando Force, equipped with 25 transports, 150 Waco CG–4A gliders, liaison aircraft, and a number of fighters and medium bombers. Operation THURSDAY was a three-pronged attack, with ground troops advancing on Myitkyina from the north and west. South of the objective, the idea was to clear an operational base in the jungle behind enemy lines, use C–47 transports and gliders to move in an Indian division, and supply them by air in the fight against Japanese troops who would be forced to turn about to meet them.

"Broadway," an open field with grass surrounded by jungle, became the landing site for some 37 gliders that dropped in on March 6, 1944. They successfully delivered more than five hundred troops, including field engineers, and a pair of light bulldozers. By the following evening, the advance party had secured the perimeter and graded a usable airstrip; after sundown, more than 70 C–47 transports and additional gliders landed under cover of darkness. Within a few days, about 120 transports were landing each night, unloading cargo, and hastily flying out to make room for the next incoming airplane. A smaller field was hacked out of the jungle not far away. By March 10, the pair of ragged airstrips had received nine thousand personnel, five hundred thousand pounds of stores, light field guns, antiaircraft units, and 1,283 mules along with 176 horses to carry supplies and ammunition through dense jungles to the columns now moving toward Myitkyina.

The advancing troops received additional supplies by airdrops from C–47s and small liaison airplanes. The latter also flew into convenient clearings to evacuate wounded soldiers. These rescue missions from dense jungle spots also relied for the first time on a group of six Sikorsky R–4 helicopters, which had been dispatched to the First Air Commando Force as a military experiment.

General Wingate died when his B–25 flew into a hillside and exploded after takeoff from Broadway on a return flight to India. But the push toward Myitkyina continued with Merrill's Marauders as the first Allied troops to reach its airstrip. Within hours, the First Commando's gliders made landings at Myitkyina with engineers and equipment to prepare the strip for C–47s and other aircraft. By dusk, transports were making arrivals and departures, despite Japanese artillery shells hitting the airstrip perimeter. In succeeding weeks the airlift provided a crucial flow of supplies, often under fire from enemy positions in the nearby jungle.

Operation THURSDAY became the most colorful airlift activity in the Pacific-Asian arena, although several additional airborne operations occurred. During July 1944, parachute troops jumped on Numfoor Island off the coast of New Guinea, only to find U.S. units from amphibious landings already in control of the airstrip marked as their objective. During the December battle for Leyte in the Philippines, gun crews with a 75-mm artillery battery were dropped on a ridge to cover the advance of ground units, but only one transport was assigned for this mission. Early in 1945, the drive toward Manila on the island of Luzon included a drop of thirteen hundred men who served largely as reinforcements for a rapidly moving ground offensive.

Considerable interest focused on a subsequent parachute assault to take the island of Corregidor in Manila Bay. "The Rock," as veterans called Corregidor, had long been the symbol of the U.S. military presence in the Philippines, as well as the scene of a harrowing defense and defeat during the Japanese invasion of the Philippines in 1941. The island measured only three and one-half miles long and one and one-half miles wide. Given the tendency of airborne drops to scatter miles wide of the target, plans to parachute onto Corregidor emphasized the narrow margin of error. The drop zone itself, a parade ground and golf course, was bordered on one side by sheer cliffs dropping to the sea. The C–47s made their action runs in pairs, and the size of the drop zone required each airplane to

Paratroopers delivered by C–46 Commandos float to the rolling Philippine countryside in June 1945.

make two or three passes, with six or eight troopers jumping on each pass. Planners estimated a loss rate of 10 to 50 percent, but the target's military significance and symbolic value justified the effort. In February 1945, after the first one thousand men were dropped, with 25 percent casualties, the paratroopers pinned down a number of enemy troops and provided covering fire for amphibious assaults in their sector. The battle to secure Corregidor took more weeks of vicious fighting.

The final paratroop action in the Pacific campaign occurred on February 17, 1945, when a company of the 11th Airborne jumped into the area around a large prison camp near Manila and helped liberate some two thousand internees and military personnel who had survived harsh captivity since the fall of the Philippines in 1942.

LEGACIES

Airborne operations resulted in some of the most dramatic missions of the Second World War. Despite the difficulties of inserting large numbers of paratroops into a compact area and of tenuous logistics and supply, airborne surprise attack continued to be employed throughout the conflict. Although Allied airborne forces around Caen and Utah Beach in France played a special role in the Normandy invasion, airborne attacks never

This C–47 Skytrain crew carried 81-mm mortar shells, oil, gas, food, and clothing to Luzon in the Philippines.

seemed to be as decisive as mission planners had hoped. Nonetheless, airborne forces developed a formidable fighting reputation, not only in initial paratroop drops but also as part of the regular ground forces while fighting continued.

Airborne assaults proved far more successful in the CBI theater, where dense jungle and rugged terrain—plus command of the air—added to the element of surprise for the attacking forces and blunted the defender's ability to mount a counteroffensive. Additionally, the AAF supplied many of the air transports that participated in combined operations with British forces in Burma and on the Malay Peninsula. These aerial sorties proved effective in maintaining ongoing British offensives even when Japanese forces appeared to threaten them. But the Japanese, at the end of a long, overland logistical tail, often faltered in the face of determined Allied airlift assets.

Statistically, the ATC emerged from the war a veritable powerhouse. By August 1945, troop strength reached 209,201 military personnel, plus 104,667 civilians. The ATC fleet of thirty-seven hundred aircraft operated an aerial network stretching 180,000 miles, reaching virtually everywhere in the world. The ATC's activities had changed intercontinental air travel from a state of high-risk adventure to a matter of daily routine. At its peak of operations, ATC aircraft crossed the Atlantic at an average rate of one every thirteen minutes. In the process, the time required to cover distances around the world shrank dramatically, from a matter of weeks to a few days or, within a theater, to a few hours.

Before the war, American Airlines fielded one of the largest aviation transport fleets in the United States, with about seventy-nine airplanes. In the postwar era the size of all airlines in the United States increased. The experience of tracking the far-flung routes of the ATC and of building and managing its complex infrastructure made postwar challenges seem far less daunting. C. R. Smith's air fleet numbered several hundred after the war, with more elaborate commercial routes, more personnel, and more four-engine airplanes. The airline benefited from Smith's ATC experience, and other airlines realized similar benefits from their wartime service. The smoothly running operations of airline routes in the United States and around the globe represented a significant legacy in terms of well-trained managers and the many TCC and ATC fliers and navigators who piloted civil transports on routes they had helped develop during wartime. Highly trained mechanics, meteorologists, electronics specialists, and other personnel also found employment with the airlines. And the many wartime airfields scraped out around the rims of the Atlantic and Pacific Oceans could and would be used by postwar civil transports—yet another benefit of airlift technology as it evolved during World War II.

Wartime operations certainly demonstrated the value of airlift assets. Civil airliner designs continued to equip many squadrons during the early postwar years, but it had become clear that the AAF needed specific kinds of aircraft designed expressly to fulfill military airlift missions. Even before the end of World War II, aeronautical firms began addressing these requirements with twin-engine and four-engine transports. Fairchild's proposal for the C–82 Packet marked a new era of dedicated military trans-

The Fairchild XC–82's clamshell rear door made loading heavy cargo easy and parachute drops faster and safer.

ports. Based on wartime reports, the Fairchild design tried to maximize ease of loading and unloading both troops and bulky cargo and to facilitate the efficient delivery of paratroopers into the battlefield. To these ends, Fairchild engineers laid out a twin-engine airplane with a central fuselage nacelle to carry crew, cargo, and personnel. Shoulder-mounted wings and engines provided low ground clearance for easy loading, with twin tail booms stretching back to the tail assembly. This layout permitted oversized, clamshell doors at the rear of the fuselage nacelle, facilitating the loading of heavy equipment such as field guns, light tanks, and trucks up to a weight of 11,500 pounds. As a troop carrier, the C–82 handled forty-two equipped paratroopers, and had a range of nearly four thousand miles with a top speed of 250 mph. The clamshell doors at the rear of the fuselage also permitted faster, safer parachute drops. The C–82 made its first flight in the autumn of 1944, but delivery of production models did not occur until September 1945, after the war's end. Nonetheless, the Packet and its more famous successor, the C–119 Flying Boxcar (or Dollar-Nineteen), introduced in 1947, eventually set new standards for airlift operations.

A new generation of four-engine transports was planned for intercontinental airlift. The first of these—the Douglas C–74 Globemaster—aggressively advertised its intended role through its name. Work on the Globemaster began early in the war, especially in anticipation of airlift requirements to come during the Pacific campaign. The design promised impressive performance for its day, cruising at around 300 mph and capable of missions spanning seventy-eight hundred miles. Military specifica-

Fairchild C–82s drop parachuted howitzers for use by ground forces.

The Douglas C–124 Globemaster II missed World War II but served strategic postwar needs.

tions called for the airplane to carry 125 combat-equipped soldiers or 115 stretchers for medical service. The C–74 was required to carry sixty thousand pounds of cargo and featured a self-contained loading system that used an electric elevator built into the center of the airplane's cargo deck. The Douglas transport also housed a compartment for a galley, chef, and a relief crew for duty on longer flights. The prototype first flew several days after the end of World War II and the cancellation of wartime contracts resulted in a production run of only 14 aircraft. Nonetheless, the airplane's size and impressive capability, plus strategic needs of the Cold War era, led to the Douglas C–124 Globemaster II. The new transport used the wing design, tail unit, and engine installations of its predecessor, and a production run of 448 airplanes led to several improved models capable of hauling seventy-four thousand pounds of cargo. With radar and clamshell doors in the nose, C–124 transports introduced a new era in versatility and productivity.

Wartime experience and modern equipment supported many significant airlift operations in the postwar years. The Berlin Airlift of 1948–49 involved both military and civil aircraft. "Limited conflicts," such as those that took place in Korea (1950–53) and Vietnam (1964–74), relied heavily on intercontinental and in-theater airlifts. Moreover, civil aviation supported national security requirements during World War II, contributing aircraft and personnel. Efforts to formalize this arrangement lagged until 1952, when the Civil Reserve Aircraft Fleet (CRAF) became a legal entity. The program committed funds of several million dollars over the intervening years to ensure that reinforced floors and cargo decks were built into a specified number of commercial aircraft that would be on call for the Air

Force. During the Gulf War of 1990–91, some 150 CRAF aircraft served military operations, delivering as much as 25 percent of the air cargo and 60 percent of personnel arriving by air.

As a national security asset, military airlift in the postwar era continued to demonstrate the values it pioneered during World War II.

SUGGESTED READING

Barry, Gregory, and John Batchelor. *Airborne Warfare, 1918–1945.* New York: Exeter Books, 1979.

Cave, Hugh B. *Wings Across the World: The Story of the Air Transport Command.* New York: Dodd, Mead, 1945.

Conley, Manuel. "Whispering Wings." *Aviation Quarterly* VII (1984): 264–80.

Craven, Wesley Frank, and James Lea Cate, eds. *The Army Air Forces in World War II.* Vol. I, *Plans and Early Operations, January 1939 to August 1942.* Chicago: University of Chicago Press, 1948. New imprint by the Office of Air Force History, 1983.

———. *The Army Air Forces in World War II.* Vol. VII, *Services Around the World.* Chicago: University of Chicago Press, 1958. New imprint by the Office of Air Force History, 1983.

Dmitri, Ivan. *Flight to Everywhere.* New York: McGraw-Hill, 1944.

Gavin, James M. *Airborne Warfare.* Washington, D.C.: Infantry Journal Press, 1947.

Hickey, Michael. *Out of the Sky: A History of Airborne Warfare.* New York: Scribner's, 1979.

La Farge, Oliver. *The Eagle in the Egg.* Boston: Houghton Mifflin, 1949.

McAuliffe, Kathleen. "Crossing the Lines in Silent Wings." *Smithsonian Magazine* 25 (June 1994): 118–33.

McDonald, Charles. *Airborne.* New York: Ballantine, 1970.

Military Airlift Command History Office. *Anything, Anywhere, Anytime: An Illustrated History of the Military Airlift Command, 1941–1991.* Scott AFB, Ill.: HQ MAC, 1991.

Mrazek, James, E. *Fighting Gliders of World War II.* New York: St. Martin's Press, 1977.

Munson, Kenneth. *Helicopters and Other Rotorcraft Since 1907.* New York: Macmillan, 1968.

Pearcy, Arthur. *DE–3*. New York: Ballantine, 1975.

Sears, Stephen. "Hell's Highway to Arnhem," in Stephen Sears, ed., *World War II: The Best of American Heritage*. New York: Houghton Mifflin, 1991.

Serling, Robert J. *Eagle: The History of American Airlines*. New York: St. Martin's Press, 1985.

Spencer, Otha C. *Flying the Hump: Memories of an Air War*. College Station: Texas A&M University Press, 1992.

Tunner, William H. *Over the Hump*. New York: Duell, 1964.

U.S. Secretary of War. *The United States Strategic Bombing Survey: Air Operations in China, Burma, India, WWII*. Washington, D.C.: U.S. Government Printing Office, 1947.

Young, Warren R. *The Helicopters*. Alexandria, Va.: Time-Life Books, 1982.

www.ingramcontent.com/pod-product-compliance
Lightning Source LLC
Chambersburg PA
CBHW060820090426
42738CB00002B/53